HARRY HILL'S TV BURP BOOK

EBURY
PRESS

INTRODUCTION BY PRINCE CHARLES

Clarence House | London W1

Winter 2009

Dear Reader,

There's no doubt about it that I like a laugh!

We all do in the Royal Family – from my famous Goon impressions to the Royal It's A Knockout we did in the 80's, to Prince Philip's slightly racist jokes, to my own son Prince Harry's hilarious Nazi impressions, talk about a bunch of Duchy Originals!!!

I think we have established that the House of Windsor is Britain's First Family of Comedy.

Often when the worries of global warming and modern architecture start to press on my brain and I start to get one of my headaches which only one of Camilla's special 'below waist' massages will shift (not that! Lumbar spine, you oaf!) I might get one of my footmen to turn on the television for me. What a wonderful device it is! With its pretty colours and tiny people going about their business. I particularly enjoy You've Been Framed* in which an old lady falls down at a wedding and we can see her knickers, or a kitten falls off a draining board into a swing bin... which reminds me I must send in that clip I've got of Mama up at Sandringham at the Christmas do. Oh, and that one of Grannie walking into a closed patio door with a tray of drinks. Anyway it was through You've Been Framed that I first became aware of comedian turned doctor Harry Hill, who provides the commentary to this my favourite show.

*Not You've Been Framed, but his other show TV Burp

NEVER HEARD OF IT, SORRY. P.C.

I have since awarded it a Prince's Trust award as I believe for the half hour it is on (or a whole hour on a bank holiday or Boxing Day) it gives young people something to do which I think is so important in these hurly burly times of Internet porn, cheap wine from Tesco and a Kentucky Fried Chicken bargain bucket (sounds like the perfect night in – says Camilla! Not really, just another example of my crazy sense of humour!!!).

So it is with great pleasure that I declare this You've Been Framed Annual open for business!

Yours sincerely

Prince Charles.

HRH The Prince of Wales
(Sausage manufacturer)

HARRY HILL
Of London

Hello There!

... and welcome to this, my first TV Burp book, an in-depth appraisal of the current state of British TV, covering socioeconomic trends, age and culture demographics, impact of technological advancements and also taking the mick out of TV.

In a world where the banks have collapsed, where children terrorise pensioners on the streets with their hand-held electronic devices and man fights woman in the home for possession of the TV remote control, it's nice to know that we can depend on TV to provide us with a mirror by which to gauge ... er ... (*"How am I doing?"* – Harry. *"Keep going"* – The Publisher).

Surely by watching shows like Big Brother, Freaky Eaters, The Apprentice and Top Of The Pops (*"That's not on any more!"* – P. *"Isn't it? What's that programme with people singing and Lenny Henry's in the audience?"* – H. *"You're thinking of Later With Jool's Holland"* – P.) Surely by watching Later With Jools Holland and shows like that we are able to see people singing ... um ... as Lenny Henry watches and maybe chats to Duffy.

In a world where ... in an uncertain world where a man can be fined for parking his car in the wrong place, as judged by a tiny man in a yellow box with a camera, where a Member of Parliament is sneered at for claiming money from the taxpayer for the essential work of having his moat cleaned out by a Labour supporter, where dogs are fined for fouling the footpath even though they are unable to carry money on them, a world where Chris Tarrant is able to pretend to go fishing when really he is in a secret house down the road wearing a beard and dressed as a woman ... Where is the love? I hear you cry! Where is the love, Harry? Who killed love? (*"Where's this going?"* – P. *"Not sure"* – H.)

Well, let me tell you that love is alive and well and is in your hands now, because each page of this book has been infused with love, not the primitive, carnal love that Chris Tarrant has for his fish, not the front-page love Lembit Opik has for a Cheeky Girl – No! The sweet and endearing love of a father for his child, of a mummy golden retriever for her newborn pup (*"This is dynamite!"* – P. *"Thanks!"* – H.) The sort of love a Tory MP has for his moat, or Melvyn Bragg has for a flagship arts programme on ITV and, dear reader, the sort of love that an author has for his most precious book.

You hold it in your hands now, that love, freshly delivered, its pages recently wet – not from amniotic fluid, but from printer's ink – the very lifeblood of book printing. Lo! How it kicks its little legs and looks up into your adoring eyes, this book; go on – tickle its tummy! Caress its spine, but most of all turn its pages and let the love out.

Somewhere a real baby is born, a mother's work is just beginning, a father, as he lights his cigar, is filled with hope for the future, and you? You have the next best thing: my TV Burp book. Congratulations! Pop open the champagne! Unwrap the Tescos finest mini pork pies and picnic eggs. But if I see it on ebay I'll flaming well kill you!

kind regards & best wishes, love

Harry Hill x♡x

Harry Hill

Author, Father, TV Addict

HESTON BLUMENTHAL'S
FUTURE OF FOOD

Fresh from his cookery lab the self-styled baldy-bonce-four-eyed-twerp chef reveals his food predictions, many of which are so far-fetched they'll cause your elbows to invert and pants to fall down!

> Using my special Tarot pans™ and studying pie charts and food trends, I, Heston Blumenthal, am able to share with you now my food predictions.

> I have seen the future of food and it ain't just tablets!

Carrot

Chicken Legs — HFC

SALTYPEPPER™

Salt and pepper in one canister. OK this is a fairly low-key food prediction but I reckon Saltypepper™ is gonna be the must-have condiment for the two thousand and teens. This is how it works: a canister, right? With salt and pepper mixed together inside it so that you will no longer have to apply salt and then pepper (or pepper and then salt), but just the one shake – dispensing salt and pepper at the same time. Got it? No? OK Well, you know when someone gives you your dinner and there's not enough salt or pepper on it? Yeah? OK, at the moment you need two different dispensers don't you? One for salt, one for pepper. Well this way it's all in the one dispenser. Got it? Right. ("I think we've got it now, Heston" - Harry). I have already started working on my Saltypepper™ mix and submitted the necessary forms to Dragons' Den. I know what you're thinking: how many holes does it have on the top — the convention being one hole for salt and three or more holes for pepper. Well Saltypepper™ has two holes on top. Yes, just two, to avoid confusion.

GLOW IN THE DARK CHEESE

You know when you get in late, it's dark and you don't want to wake up the Mr or Mrs? That's where glow in the dark cheese comes in.
I know what you're going to say Mr Clever Pants — that's what the light inside the fridge is for ("That's what the light in the fridge is for surely?" – Harry) — for late-night snacking, but what if, like me, you took the bulb out of the fridge light to replace the bulb that blew in the glove compartmnent of your car and have ordered a new bulb but the manufacturers say it's got to come from Italy and will be three months? ("Bit far-fetched" – Harry) That's when you'll be begging me for glow in the dark cheese. What I've done is scraped the luminous paint off a number of digital watches and mixed that in with cheese to create a Stilton-like blue veiny cheese,only the veins glow in the dark. Spooky yeah? You bet. I know what you're thinking: "Doesn't luminous paint cause cancer or something?" Yes it does, you're right, so you've got to be carefulnot to eat the paint part. Once again — a teething problem. I'm also working a big ball of Edam studded with you're a chef

CLONED CHOPS

Aren't chops great? ("Particularly with a scoop of mash on the side" – Harry) But, and it's a big but, chops are notoriously variable in size aren't they? Some are thick and juicy while others are thin and dry, lacking flavour (even after the addition of Saltypepper™!!) So how about if you were able to get exactly the same chop time after time after time? Impossible? It is at the moment, but using methods that I've copied from the Jeff Goldblum film "The Fly". I'm well on the way to the chop cook's dream of cloning chops – both pork and lamb ("Beef doesn't get a chop – I don't make the rules up" - Harry. "Can you stop interrupting?" - Heston. "Sorry!" - Harry).

By connecting two microwave ovens in parallel using tin foil and a lead from my camcorder I am hoping I will be able to transfer the genetic profile of the chop in microwave a) to the chop in microwave b).

So far my results have been a little bit unpredictable. Most of the time I just get two cooked chops which I then eat because I find chops irresistible and don't want them to get cold, but once when I opened microwave b there was the usual cooked chop PLUS a dead, cooked fly – just like on the Jeff Goldblum film!! I ate the chop and I ate the fly which I noted tasted a bit like the chop. Was this chop-flavoured fly truly made from altered DNA or did it taste like that because it was on the chop and the juices from the chop had run off on to the fly? We'll never know but it's very exciting stuff. Watch this space - well not this space but the space inside microwave B. (That's a 'B' not a microwaved Bee – it was a fly that I cooked).

FREEZE-DRIED WATER

Ever find that water is a bit runny? What if you could get water in powder form? Go for that would you? You bet your sweet cockatrice you would. One day it will be possible. How do I know? Well, when you boil a pan of water down to nothing there is sometimes like a fine white deposit around the inside of the pan – well, that's powdered water. It must be, right? As I didn't add anything to the water and my assistant Igor didn't add anything either. I've been boiling up water now pretty much non-stop for ten years scraping this white stuff off a bit like Marie Curie when she came up with the recipe for radium. I collected almost a gram of it and sure enough when I diluted it with water: hey presto – water!

FOOD IN TABLET FORM

Don't fight it, it's inevitable, food one day will be in tablet form. I read about it when I was a boy growing up in the Heston Service Station and saw it on Tomorrow's World too. One day you won't need fancy cookery and sauces – it will be possible to simply pop open a pack of pills, select the flavour you want and knock it back with a slug of water. All us chefs will be on the dole again and Channel 4 will have lost half its schedule and may have to bring back Rory Bremner to plug the shortfall. Is that what you people want? Well? ("Yes!"– Harry)

What they haven't worked out is that this food pill – tiny as it is, will easily be able to slip past the gastric band that most people will have fitted by the year 2012 – thus Fern Britton, Russell Grant, royal reporter James Whittaker, Tommy Walsh et al. will start piling back on the pounds and we will be forced to watch endless rounds of Fit Club. It's a pretty bleak outlook isn't it food fans?

Bit of a down beat ending, Heston!

Yes, sorry about that but I feel quite strongly about it!

ALL IS QUIET ON THE STREET. DAVID PLATT SITS WAITING WITH HIS ELECTRIC RAZOR.

ONE DAY HAIR WILL GROW OUT OF MY FACE AND WHEN IT DOES I'LL BE READY FOR IT

AT THE WEBSTER RESIDENCE KEVIN IS DECIDING WHAT TO WEAR.

WHY OH WHY DO I BUY SO MANY SIMILAR JUMPERS FROM BHS

AT DEV ALAHAN'S PENTHOUSE FLAT HE REGRETS LAST NIGHT'S DINNER DATE.

PWOR! I KNEW I SHOULDN'T HAV TAKEN HER TO NANDO'S

AT ROY'S ROLLS BECKY IS FULL OF REMORSE.

HE SAID QUITE CLEARLY PORK SAUSAGE AND BUBBLE!

OUT ON THE ROAD THE PEOPLE OF CORONATION STREET AWAIT THE ARRIVAL OF THE EARLY MORNING TRAIN.

HERE IT COMES LOOK!

ON BOARD THE TRAIN ARE NORRIS, RITA, TONY AND CARLA.

WE SHOULD BE THERE ANY MINUTE

I'VE NEVER TRAVELLED FIRST CLASS BEFORE

AT THE ROVERS LIZ MCDONALD PERFORMS HER DAILY NIT INSPECTION.

GOOD LUCK FINDING ONE ON ME!

GOT ONE! A BIG JUICY NIT!

AGGH! CAREFUL LIZ!

AT THE PANTS FACTORY, UNDERWORLD TONY AND CARLA ARE VERY PLEASED WITH THEIR NEW RECRUIT.

GREAT IDEA TO GET LIAM CLONED CARLA!

THANKS TONY!

BUT AT THE BARLOW RESIDENCE TROUBLE IS BREWING...

OH NO BLANCHE IS TRYING TO FLUSH A WET WIPE, AGAIN AND IT'S OVERFLOWED!

KEN CONFRONTS BLANCHE ABOUT THE WET WIPE...

I DO NOT LOOK CAMP!

IT'S A MACERATOR SYSTEM BLANCHE, IT CAN ONLY COPE WITH BOG PAPER!

OH LOOK PETER AND JORDAN ARE ON JEREMY KYLE!

YOU LOOK A BIT CAMP STANDING LIKE THAT, KEN.

DON'T ANSWER BACK! NAUGHTY BOY!

STUNNED BY DEIRDRE'S ASSAULT, ALL THE YEARS OF PENT-UP AGGRESSION WITHIN KEN FINALLY SURFACE... AND HE GOES ON A VIOLENT RAMPAGE. ATTACKING ANYONE HE COMES ACROSS.

FIRST YOUNG DAVID PLATT.

AAAAAAAGH!

THEN BECKY AND THE DISGRUNTLED CUSTOMER IN ROY'S ROLLS.

GERTCHA!

THEN NORRIS IN THE KABIN...

OOOOOH! ME LOLLIES!

NORRIS WHATEVER HAPPENED?

OH RITA IT ALL HAPPENED SO FAST!

DID YOU GET A GOOD LOOK AT HIM?

HAVE YOU GOT MY COPY OF NUTS?

NO, IT'S IN TUESDAY

SOMEHOW KEN HAS GAINED ACCESS TO CORONATION STREET HIGH SCHOOL AND CONTINUES HIS VIOLENT SPREE.

POW!

WHAT YOU LOOKING AT?

IT WAS KEN, AND HE WERE MAD!

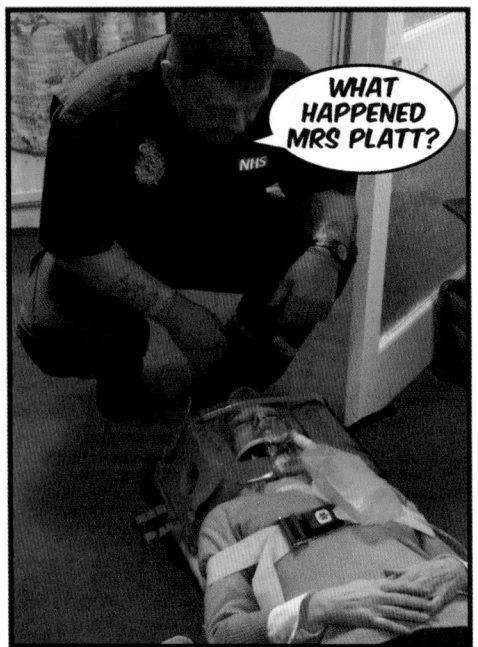

WHAT HAPPENED MRS PLATT?

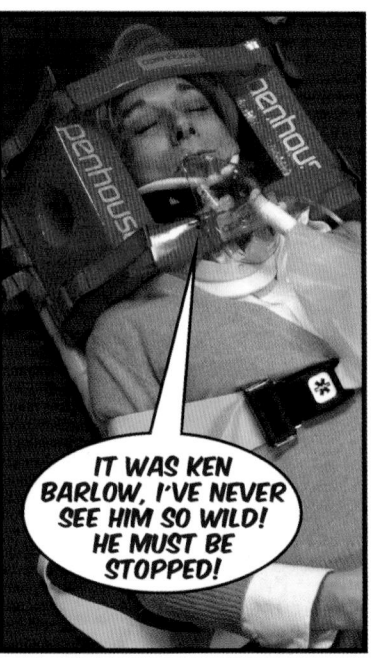

IT WAS KEN BARLOW, I'VE NEVER SEE HIM SO WILD! HE MUST BE STOPPED!

BUT KEN HAD A TASTE FOR IT NOW AND WALKED THE EARTH LUSTING FOR BLOOD.

NEED BLOOD!

THE END

YOU'VE BEEN Framed!

IN 2-D

What Happened Next?

A The old girl on the left spills her orange juice.
B The waiter trips over his own shadow.
C The old girl in blue on the chair leans back and falls through the plate-glass window showing her knickers at the same time!

What Happened Next?

A The old girl falls into the flowerbed gashing her legs on the rose thorns which later become septic and result in lockjaw.
B The house falls down due to shoddy workmanship.
C Her shoes break and she falls backwards showing her knickers.

What Happened Next?

A The man pulls out his hand to reveal a claw-like structure.
B The building collapses on top of him and he has to spend the rest of his days lying down.
C When he takes his hand out of his pocket his trousers fall down showing his pants.

What Happened Next?

A The wall falls on her.
B The tree falls on her.
C A man rides in on a quad blike (looking a bit like Ozzy Osbourne). Part of the bike gets caught on her dress and when he rides off he rips a segment of the dress off, revealing her knickers.

What Happened Next?

A The woman on the left slips forward knocking the cake on to the man's lap causing him to take his trousers off and thus revealing his pants.
B The woman on the left falls backwards revealing her knickers.
C The woman on the left threatens the man on the right, steals his wallet, then escapes on foot over the fields, showing her knickers as she kicks her legs high across the gently swaying corn. He will never see her again and will curse the day he ever got introduced to Facebook.

What Happened Next?

The man on the left's hat is blown on to the man in the middle's head.

The man on the right's hat is blown on to the man in the middle's head then up into the air. Meanwhile, the man on the left's hat is blown up into the air and on to the man on the right's head. The man on the right's original hat then lands on the man on the left's head.

The man in the middle is knocked over by a wave causing his trousers to fall down showing his pants. Then a seagull does a poo on his head.

The Adventures Of Ant and Dec...

...in their fantastic Adjoining Houses!

Chiswick, London.

The homes of Anton McPartlin and Declan McAnt – the real-life names of TV's second most popular entertainers. They used to share a house but since Anton got married their houses are now joined by a secret tunnel under the patio!

The tunnel leads to a secret fun den where the boys have all sorts of different games set up. Indoor swingball, table football and Yahtzee to name but a few!

One night.

ANT? IT'S DEC!

HELLO DEC! YES SHE'S ASLEEP. FANCY MEETING UP IN THE TUNNEL FOR A GAME OF BADMINTON?

SURE THING. I'LL MEET YOU AT THE TOP OF YOUR TUNNEL AND WE'LL GO TOGETHER TO THE DEN AS I'M A BIT FRIGHTENED TO GO BY MYSELF.

COOL!

With that Ant opens a trap door under his bedside rug to reveal a state-of-the-art trap door.

He lifts the trap and up pops Dec's head. He's made it over already!

Together they head down the rough dirt tunnel. Above them are sewer pipes carrying waste products from all over the top celebrity hangouts of Chiswick to the open waters of the Thames.

Suddenly there is an almighty roar. The boys look up to see a rabbit has gained access to the tunnel. Because they are only small lads this usually harmless mammal is quite frightening. One kick from its powerful hind legs could send them tumbling!

ROA'ARR!!

BLIMEY! A RABBIT!

YEAH AND IT LOOKS HUNGRY!

They run down a side tunnel...

...and straight into a sticky spider's web. Dec is stuck fast.

Not only that but the owner of the web, a huge spider, is not best pleased!

Ant reaches into his pocket and finds a pack of question cards from his hit Poker TV Show.

He starts to flick them at the giant arachnid. Fortunately they're laminated and really sting, especially when they hit the spider in the eyes!

Suddenly Dec starts to sob uncontrollably.

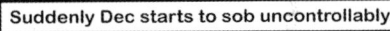

YOU SEE?! WE'VE ALWAYS HAD ADJOINING HOMES AND I'M NOT ABOUT TO LET SOMETHING LIKE A GIANT SPIDER OR RABBIT SPOIL THAT!

I S'POSE YOU'RE RIGHT, I SHOULD JUST THINK OF IT AS A BIT OF A BUSH TUCKER CHALLENGE!

YEAH WITH US AS THE TUCKER! LOOK!

Suddenly a huge frog lolloped into view

REEBIT! REEBIT!

WE'RE UP AGAINST IT NOW OLD PAL!

IT'S LIKE PAN'S LABYRINTH ALL OVER AGAIN!

YEAH, BUT WITHOUT THE SUBTITLES!

With that the frog unfurled his giant tongue and grabbed Ant.

HELP!

Dec looked around and there was the trusty old mouse from his childhood.

I HEARD YOU WERE IN TROUBLE AND CAME VIA A NETWORK OF TUNNELS ALL THE WAY FROM NEWCASTLE.

HOP ON!

So Dec hops on the rodent.

The mouse bites the frog's tongue, releasing Ant.

TAKE THAT FROGGY!!

AM I GLAD TO SEE YOU!

Then they ride on down the tunnel.

HEY ANT THIS MUST BE WHAT IT'S LIKE TO RIDE THE JIGGY BANK THAT WE GET THE PUBLIC TO DO!

YES, BUT WITHOUT THE PUBLIC HUMILIATION AND POUND COINS!

Back at the entrance to Ant's home.

THANKS MOUSEY!

NOT A PROBLEM, GUYS. KEEP IN TOUCH.

SEND OUR BEST BACK TO THE RIVER TYNE !

THE FROG ON THE TYNE ISN'T ALL MINE, ALL MINE!

SEE YOUSE TOMORROW ON SET!

WHY AYE!

Next morning.

EUGH! ANT YOU SMELL OF FROG SALIVA! WHY?

YOU WOULDN'T BELIEVE ME IF I TOLD YOU !

THE END

"I CAN SEE DEAD PEOPLE"

DEREK ACORAH'S SPOOKY TALES
(IN THE ORIGINAL SCOUSE LANGUAGE)

"You heap big star on UK Living!"

SPOOKY CASE: ___No. 1___ THE MYSTERIOUS JOLLY SAILOR

LOCATION: ___DEREK'S MUM'S HOUSE, SOUTHPORT___

TIME: ___MIDNIGHT___   DATE: ___1974___

OBSERVATIONS:

When I was a lad, like, before I was a big star on UK Livin' TV growing up with me mam in da 'pool, when the Beatles set our toes tappin' and also the Merseybeats, although, no now you come to mention it they was broke up by den, I t'ink it was 1970 in fact when da Beatles broke up. Was it dat Jap cow Yoko or woz it just four lads who'd had enough, I mean Paul had met Linda by den and George had had enough, as can be seen in da film Let It Be. Anyway, dere I was a full four years later in me mam's house, not more dan a mile from Ringo's place in Madryn Street (my cousin used to play wid dem and dey was a ruff bunch, I tell ya dat). Any road, dere we was, it were all dark, like, and I had gone a bed. I fancied a drink a water - well, come it! I was only eight like! So, I walks down da corridor and I can hear dis strange creakin' and a moaning comin' from me gran's room. A little voice in me ear told me to go and investigate (I later found out dis was Sam, me spirit guide, a Mohawk Indian dat was shot at da battle of da Little Big Horn many many years ago and who has been at me side, guidin' me like da name suggests). So I walks down de corridor to investigate, like, and I see dis like apparition of a Sailor comin' out her room. Bold as brass, looked almost like I could touch him! Well he sees me and and sets to cursin' at me, den me gran comes out lookin' all flushed like and I sez "Did you just see what I just saw?" and she said "You saw nuttin' alright? Dere's a tanner now go back to bed" and she gave me a coin of da realm. That's when I realised I could make money out of special things that only I could see.

SPOOKY CASE: ___No. 2___ THE CAR THAT WAS ALIVE

LOCATION: ___LAY-BY, OFF JUNCTION 4, M1___

TIME: ___2 AM___   DATE: ___1986___

OBSERVATIONS:

Before I got on da TV, like, I used to have to go round doin' me act in a lot of pubs, like in me Nissan Sunny dat me grandma left me. Dat was a gear car dat was! And da number plate was DLT 4RS and I contacted Dave Lee Travis's people to see if he like was interested cos that's a personalised number plate for him, sort of if the 4 and the R and the S meant something too (I reckoned dey was his special psychic numbers, like we all have, and if you wanna find out what yours is send us a fiver and I'll stick it in da post like). Anyway I never heard back from DLT the scally and him from up north too, where we look after our own. Still, what's he doin' now eh? Dave Lee flaming Travis (well he popped up on TV's Naughtiest Blunders de udder day with Michaela Strachan, and it was a riot I laffed me head off, nice guy!).

Anyway, dere I was in da Nissan flyin' up da M1 after one of me mindreading acts in a pub in Watford (thirty quid cash and drinks for free) - and the flamin' big end went! Smoke pourin' out of da bonnet and no sign of anyone. Well I didn't have insurance like, and be fair I'd had a drink. So I tink I'd better just dump da car, de old wreck! and see if I can hitch like, dat's right stick me tum out - like Macca at a press launch! And try me tum at 'itchin'! I starts walking up da slip road and come upon a like a layby and dere it was! A car, right, some old hatchback, looked like a Metro but coulda been a Maestro da lights were out on it yet it was bouncin' up and down - all by itself! I couldn't believe me blueys! Well I was dead scared, but I don't know what it was I was somehow drawn to it - maybe it was me psychic power pulling me in dere or, I dunno what, then I hears Sam, me spirit guide egging me on like "Go on Derek, have a look in da car! See what youse can see. Heap big ghost might be in there!!" (that's right he's Mohawk). As I got closer I could see a ghostly mist all up da windows and that same moaning that was coming from me mam's room, that night she had the sailor round! As I looked in - and me hands were shakin' I were that terrified I saw da ghostly face of a woman, looked to me like Gillian Taylforth, but was obviously someone from da spirit world. De spirit cussed at me again, shockin' words from da spirit! And I made me way back on to the road. Slept the night in da car, made me way to da services da next day and got me stepbrother to pick me up in da Transit. But what a spooky night eh?

OBSERVATIONS:

Big jump now in da time line and I'm now a big star like, on da TV like but I didn't forget me mam up in da 'pool, no as soon as I got me first pay packet like, off UK Livin', I bought me mam a puppy, from one o' dem puppy farms, like and sent it up to her in da 'pool. Unfortunately by da time it got to her it had entered da spirit world, yeah shame dat, s'pose I shoulda put a few holes in da Jiffy bag. No, come it I'm jokin' youse, I put plenty a holes in da Jiffy bag but she was out when dey delivered it and dey left it at a friend's house who forgot to 'and it over, like. By da time me mam got back from Hamburg da poor little mite had snuffed it. Still, he's in spirit and I daresay I might see 'im on one o' me shows. Anyway forget dat! Dis ain't about dat! No, as I say I'm a big star for UK Livin' TV, having ditched dem losers off Most Haunted, cos I wasn't gettin' a proper look in like was I? Dat cow (NAME) she was hoggin' it so I tought, Hang on Derek, I tought Hang on Derek, youse is bigger dan dis show, and me spirit guide, Sam he said it to me as well, he said "Hang on a minute Derek, see if youse can land youse self your own show, like, you gonna be heap big star." So anyways, I came up with Derek Acorah's (That's me) Ghost Towns where I goes around like da towns and people get me in to get rid of people who are in spirit who are producin' bad energies. First dey tell da researchers all about da bad spirit and what da problem is, plus a little local history - which of course I never get to see, unless me spirit guide Sam - naughty as he is, uses my body as a vehicle to sneak into da producer's office and print it off his laptop in da night after everyone's gone 'ome.

Any road up wid me new fame comes a loada dough dat you can pick up doin' like dese corporates? Personal appearances, yeah students' venues, night clubs, shoppin' centres, dat type a ting. Well one of dem was dis Heaven Night Club, under da railway arches near da Embankment in London. Now don't get me wrong, like any scouser I hates Cocknees, 'cept for Jamie Oliver who, fair play to 'im has tried to get us Northerners to give up chips. And Gary Rhodes is alright too - Antony Worrall Thompson I can take him or leave him but I met 'im once at a corporate at Newbury race course and he was nice as pie, den I found out he was a lookalike - da scab!

Any road I turns up to dis Heaven place and dey must a had a very strict dress code! First up dey was all blokes, nuttin' wrong wid dat I love lads and let's all have a bevvy on a Friday down da pub. Dere dey was den all da guys dancin' on da dance floor to disco tracks - in fact I t'ought I saw Sam, me Mohawk spirit guide on da stage singin' YMCA but no it was somethin' to do with a bunch called da Village People. So I'm introduced - da star of Livin' TV's Ghost Towns, Derek Acorah and I goes on. Bit of a mute response to be honest, bit disappointin' considerin' I'd travelled all dat way from me mam's house up da M1. But I make da best of it, I get someone up and talk to 'em like and go into one o' me trancelike states and contact dere dead cousin who overdosed on glue and I only found out it was da producer of Ghost Towns later - I swear to God, I didn't know, it was dark like, I swear on Sam me spirit guide's life dat I never knew and I don't pay him to be in da audience. Any road I'd say I got about a t'ird of dem's attention the rest were carrying on dancin'. Sam whispers in me ear, "Blow dis for a lark, you might as well get bevvied." So I went up da bar. Well, dey've only got dis soft southern bottled beer like, but I like dat, and much of it is produced up north anyways so I gets hammered, me and Sam. I'm drinking lager, he's following dem up with shorts. After a while I needs to go a loo. I makes me way to da gents and I don't know about you but I don't like da urinals, can't go, I feel all self conscious like, any road I approach da cubicle and would ya believe it, it's a cubicle for one like, but dere's two voices comin' out of it! I puts me face right up against it and says "Who's dere!" and da spirits inside set to cussin' me out, foul-mouthed dey was! Oh dey turned da air blue with four-letter expletives, so I made me excuses and left.

But what a spooky night dat was!

TV SHOWS TO WAT

"I got my guys on the inside to leak out a few details of what's on the cards for next year and you won't believe your eyes!"

CASH IN THE ATTIC
PAUL BURRELL SPECIAL

Paul shows us some of the goodies that he's got in his loft and under the floorboards of his flower shop in Chester. He knows that if Australian Princess gets cancelled he's got a pension plan right there!

RICKY GERVAIS'S
HEROES OF MONEY

The portly star of Extras and the 11 o'Clock Show talks to some of the wealthy people he's hooked up with since he got famous such as Ben Stiller, David Bowie, Baron Philippe de Rothschild and Serbian warlord Radovan Karadzic. He talks with them about investments and future plans he has for his money.

DAVID BECKHAM'S
TATTOO SCHOOL

David takes us behind the scenes at the special Institute of tattooing that he's set up to give underprivileged kids a chance to get a tattoo. Meet eight-year-old Leon, whose mum has gone to Spain for the summer on holiday, leaving him with his six-month-old half-brother TK Max. Watch as David arranges for him to get a tattoo saying 'Mum' in Chinese (we think) and a picture of a nude woman then puts his baby half-brother in for a big one of Tupac. Heartrending, feelgood stuff.

TONIGHT
WITH TREVOR McDONALD
PETE DOHERTY SPESHAL (sic)

Maintaining his unswerving nose for a story and the impeccable journalistic approach that has seen him sweep the board at the TV Kwik awards, ITV's jewel in the curry, Sir Trevor McDonald, goes behind the scenes on the new Pixar Animation, which tells the touching story of the Babyshambles story – the drugs, the songs and the blood paintings.

WORLD PREMIERE:
LIVE ACTION MUPPET MOVIE
(Working title)

The people who bought you the live action (tha real actors, dummy!) version of the Thunderbir sprinkle their Midas dust on the Muppets wi an all-star cast playing the Muppets in th latest caper.

Miss Piggy - MICHAEL BALL
Kermit - PHILLIP SCHOFIELD
Fozzy Bear - PATRICK MOWER
Gonzo - MICHAEL WINNER
Statler & Waldorf - JONATHAN WILKES & LISA RILE

Promises to be even better than the St Trinia re-make.

MILL ON THE FLOSS

Catch up on the latest dental techniques wi Heather Mills. First episode – interdental brushes

CELEBRITY WHO WANTS
TO BE A MILLIONAIRE
RAMADAN SPECIAL

Join some of Britain's most prominent Muslims f this one-off millionaire special. Confirmed so far a Cat Stevens, Abu Hamza, Prince Charles, t Archbishop of Canterbury and Kym Marsh, b watch this space!

JIMMY CARR'S BEFORE AND AFTER
THEY WERE FAMOUS

One-off show concentrating on famous people b not during the period when they were famous. Lo of funny home videos played long to pad it out.

WINSTON CHURCHILL'S
1990s IN BLACK AND WHITE

Rare old footage from the 1930s of the 1990s th has lain hidden in Winston Churchill's house f over seventy years. The decade when The Fa Show was king, Nelson Mandela met the Spic Girls, cloning was invented, Britpop was at i height and West Coast G-Funk made its debut – a seen through the eyes of the prime minister wh saw Britain through the Second World War Winston S. Churchill. Includes padding interview with Stuart Maconie, Miranda Sawyer and Bar Bulsara (né George).

OUT FOR IN 2010

[H]OW BAD IS YOUR BREATH?

[To]ny Blackburn and Pete Burns host this series of [t]welve shows where people are taken into the [st]reet and asked to breathe over babies. A cry-[o]meter measures the intensity of their response [an]d thus how bad the breath is. Featuring great [se]xual chemistry between the two hosts and tears [al]ong the way from people with terminal gum [di]sease. One lucky winner gets a full set of veneers [an]d hair highlights.

[H]OW MURDERED IS YOUR WIFE?

[Ki]m and Aggie visit houses where there has been a [co]mplaint about the smell. Could it be a dead body? [W]atch as they get permission to dig up the patio [an]d marvel as they clean up after a female adult [c]aucasian with just half a lemon each. A bit dark [b]ut great telly !

[P]IERS MORGAN'S [N]ATIONAL BRITISH PRIDE [O]F PROUDNESS AWARDS

[P]ride has never been more popular and that's why [w]e're honouring it with its own awards ceremony [c]elebrating the proudest people in Britain, presided [o]ver by the King of Pride, the much-loved [e]ntertainer Piers Morgan. Hear about the couple [w]ho were too proud to claim benefits and so [b]ecame homeless through pride. Pride levels are [m]onitored by Piers's own patented Pride-O-Meter, [w]hich measures the audience's oohs and aaahs. If [y]ou're unneccessarily proud you might be eligible [t]o enter online and through premium-rate phone [li]nes or by accosting Piers in the street.

[N]IGEL MARVEN'S [C]ASHPOINT WATCH

[T]op twitcher and peeping tom (though not proved) [N]igel Marven hides behind a specially installed [c]ashpoint machine and tries to copy down your PIN [n]umber. This information is fed back to Neil [a]"Doctor" Fox in the studio where the audience, and [y]ou at home, get a chance to "Win the PIN" and [w]ithdraw cash from someone else's account. [N]aughty but nice!

[G]OK WAN'S I'VE GOT ONE!

[F]ishing series with the Asian/Scouse fashion [d]esigner.

ANT, DEC 'N' DENISE SING THE ADVERTS

Britain's second favourite entertainers invite the audience to sing the advert jingles such as "Oooh Danone!" and "Treseme – Pure and Simple" to win favours off Denise Van Outen or Lee Mead. Special guests on week one: the girls from Sheila's Wheels.

ANDREW MARR'S BRITAIN FROM THE SIDE

Andrew Marr gets a cab round the British Isles, describes what he sees and we pay the fare and hotel bills, including mini-bar.

YOU'VE NOT BEEN FRAMED AS MUCH AS FILMED HAVING A PRANK PLAYED ON YOU

More foreign footage from the 90s with the date pixillated out, of people doing mildly amusing things as Harry Hill tries to punch up the laugh count by describing the decor or pretending they look like someone famous.

SOME SERIOUS CHANNEL 4 DOCUMENTARIES THAT ARE IN THE PIPELINE

Channel 4 kick off with a whole raft of serious looks in to yukky medical diseases and malformations.

Ouch! My Leg is Falling Off!
in-depth look at leprosy

Eugh! Look At His Head It's All Swollen!
in-depth look at birth defects

I Am The Hunchback Of Notre Dame
in-depth look at scoliosis of the spine

Blimey There's Two Of 'Em!
in-depth look at conjoined twins

Help! I Can't Do One!
in-depth look at constipation

Oi! Pinocchio! I Bet When You Do The Back Stroke Someone Shouts Shark!
in-depth look at someone whose nose is slightly bigger than average

Christ You're Ugly! I Bet When You Was Born The Midwife Slapped Your Mum!
in-depth look at a girl who is not classically good-looking

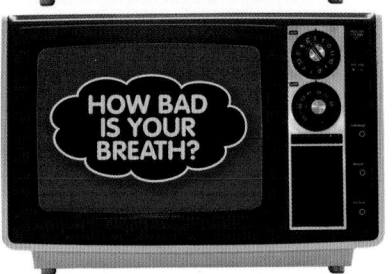

NATIONAL TV AWARDS AFTER SHOW PARTY
(KEY OVERLEAF)

NATIONAL TV AWARDS AFTER SHOW PARTY KEY

1. Gordon Ramsay and Anthony Worrall Thomspon have a stand-off – Janet Street Porter tries to break it up.
2. Dale Winton jives on the dance floor with Cilla and Paul O'Grady, whilst Adrian Chiles tries to get in on it.
3. Tana Ramsay nervously texts Victoria Beckham to make sure they're still friends.
4. Piers Morgan smooches Anne Robinson.
5. Catherine Tate enjoys a slow dance with Michael Grade.
6. Ant and Dec do the twist with each other as Ant's wife looks boredly on.
7. The cast of The Bill discuss upcoming story lines.
8. Tony Stamp (of The Bill) remains aloof and chats animatedly to Barbara Windsor about the possibility of getting on to The Square.
9. Queuing for the toilets are: Davina, Alan Carr, Kevin Spacey, Judy Finnigan and Rhino from Gladiators.
10. Ross Kemp arrives back from the Spar with some cans and cracks one open with McFadden and Brian from Big Brother.
11. Conga – Trevor McDonald, Lawrence McGinty, Raggy Omah, John Simpson, Kate Adie, Adam Boulton and Anna Botting.
12. Ian Hislop breakdances to cheers from Denise Van Outen and Lee Mead, Connie Fisher and Jack P. Shepherd from Corrie.
13. EastEnders' Billy Mitchell chats to Lord Richard Attenborough about the making of Gandhi.
14. The Top Gear table give David Attenborough the bumps. Ninety-one of them, though he laughs through gritted teeth.
15. Paul Gambaccini compares notes on recent corporate engagements with David "Kid" Jensen.
16. Sir David Jason is bugged by David Tennant, who begs him to say "you plonker Rodney".
17. Having missed the dinner, Judi Dench furtively scoffs on a bag of Monster Munch under the table while Kevin Spacey keeps an eye out for paps.
18. Lynda La Plante changes into her swimsuit behind a human screen formed by Nick Knowles, Nick Ross and Nicky Campbell.

FROM BBC3! FREAKY EATERS
WORD SEARCH

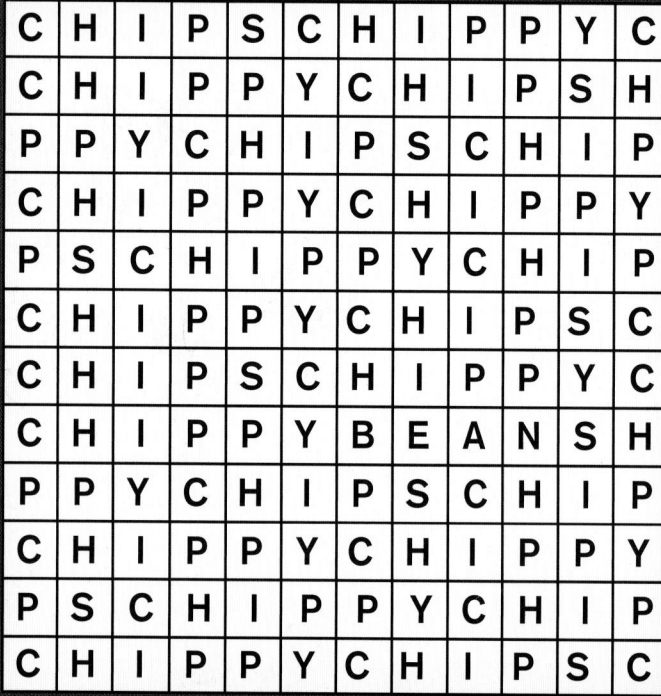

C	H	I	P	S	C	H	I	P	P	Y	C
C	H	I	P	P	Y	C	H	I	P	S	H
P	P	Y	C	H	I	P	S	C	H	I	P
C	H	I	P	P	Y	C	H	I	P	P	Y
P	S	C	H	I	P	P	Y	C	H	I	P
C	H	I	P	P	Y	C	H	I	P	S	C
C	H	I	P	S	C	H	I	P	P	Y	C
C	H	I	P	P	Y	B	E	A	N	S	H
P	P	Y	C	H	I	P	S	C	H	I	P
C	H	I	P	P	Y	C	H	I	P	P	Y
P	S	C	H	I	P	P	Y	C	H	I	P
C	H	I	P	P	Y	C	H	I	P	S	C

Too many chips may form a massive ball in your tummy and lead to so-called Ballcock Syndrome where the chip ball blocks the outflow of your stomach, and can only be shifted by cocking your leg like a dog at regular twenty-minute intervals (Fig. 1).

Fig. 1

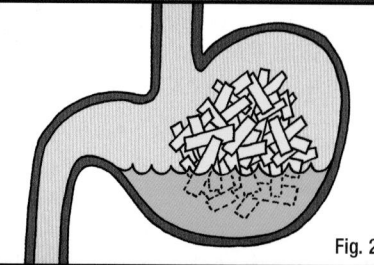

Fig. 2

If the leg goes uncocked and the stomach unemptied a cocktail of powerful enzymes and acids build up (Fig. 2) that could destroy the planet if sicked up – a bit like the Alien's blood on the first Alien film where it dissolves through the metal floor of the spaceship. Eventually this chip ball will work its way out of your stomach, get into the ventilation system of your home and reproduce, waiting to attach itself to your face and repeat its hideous life cycle.

PREVENTION
Broccoli spears, soya bean milk and frozen potato Funny Faces.

A STAR IN THE HAND!
IS WORTH TWO IN THE BUSH!

See if you can name the celebrity couples behind these bushes...

A

B

C

D

E

F

Hugh Fearnley-Whittingstall

SAYS

"YOU CAN DO IT!"

REARING LIVESTOCK AT HOME

What makes me mad, more mad than seeing a squid lying run over by the side of the road uneaten, its ink sploshed up a wall, more mad even than a chicken not being allowed to fly, to soar and reach its full potential amongst the other birds before being made into mini kievs, is when people say that animal husbandry is all very well but is not open to the ordinary man or woman in the street. I believe that good food should be available to all! Just because you live in a pokey one-bedroomed council flat doesn't mean you can't raise and rear livestock of your own. This is why I set out to prove it with my series Hugh's River Cottage High Rise Oxen in which I encouraged ordinary people like you to buy an ox calf and rear it, mate it off with another cow then slaughter it, the subsequent meat then cooked for local dignitaries and celebs – and all in a one-bedroom high-rise flat on an inner-city sink estate.

Day One

Fig. 87.—The Pork-butcher (*Charcutier*).—Fac-simile of a Miniature in a Charter of the Abbey of Solignac (Fourteenth Century).

Start to get organised and mobilise public opinion.

I write to my MP asking them to consider an 'ox allowance' in which pensioners and the disabled are given money to rear cattle in their homes. They do it with fuel bills – so why not for farming? No wonder these giant superstores like Tesco and Morrisons have an advantage. I wouldn't mind but none of them are stocking my yoghurts either (OK they're three pound apiece but come on! they're organic, what do you expect?). I decide to write to my MP about this too.

Also dash off a letter to the boss of Sainsburys to ask him why he's not stocking my yoghurts and also ask whether he'd like to come to our end-of-series car park barbecue when I'll be using the meat that has been grown in the flats.

Also call up Jamie Oliver to see if he can help as this is the sort of show he does and indeed I got the idea for it when I was watching his show where he managed to ban school dinners and children's TV in a single six-part series. Nice one J!

Also I think about planning a publicity stunt. Maybe I can persuade one of my staff to dress up as a pantomime cow and parade up and down in front of my local Tesco.

Day Two

Jamie Oliver has phoned back warning me off, saying he's doing something similar where he's trying to get OAPs to rear pigs and use the dung to power their disability vehicles. That's not fair really is it? He says if I go ahead his next programme will be dissing my yoghurts. What a bummer!

Raw squid in anchovy sauce for lunch with doughnut for pudding – scrummy! The doughnut cheered me up. On a sugar and ink high, I fax Prince Charles requesting an emergency meeting to discuss my plans. Got a very favourable response from his equerry. Unfortunately His Royal Highness is visiting an eco hotel, on his yacht in Bermuda. Rotten luck on my part. Talk to one of my farm workers, Jan, and tell him he's got to dress up as a cow and campaign outside Tesco with me, handing out leaflets telling people to watch the show and also get Tesco to stock my yoghurts. He doesn't seem happy about it but I tell him he will have to go back to Poland if he doesn't as I will tell the Home Office that he is an illegal immigrant. Why don't people want to get involved? It's really very disheartening.

Pigeons' hearts' in a liquorice sauce and cavy blood jus for dinner. Wife took me to one side and asked whether she might be allowed to cook occasionally. Fitful night burping up the squid ink from earlier mixed with the cavy blood.

Day Three

Good news! Got a cheque through from Channel 4!

I don't know how other farmers manage without these handouts from broadcasters. Write letter to Darcus Howe to see if he wants to come to the car park barbecue we're having at the end of the series. Also write to Jodie Marsh and Lembit Opik, just to be on the safe side.

It looks like the producer has found a good really run-down estate for us to film on – burnt-out cars, big drug problem, and knife crime – super!

Send Jan off to Tescos in the cow outfit with a box of leaflets.

Spit roasted a chaffinch then ate it with home-made guacamole between two thick wedges of parsnip bread, a handful of pick'n'mix (from Woolies, last time I went up to town) for pudding – delish!

Jamie Oliver arrives with that pig farmer mate of his – Jimmy. They were wearing masks but I could tell it was them. They smashed the windows in the farmhouse with baseball bats and spray painted one of the horses with the slogan "Keep OFF Our TV Ideas!". But I'm not going to be put off. Without the TV I'd have to farm this place like normal! Forget it!

Producer goes down to the council estate in South London where we're going to do my experiment and hands out leaflets with details of my plan for ordinary people to rear cattle in their high-rise flats and with details of a public meeting tomorrow. He gets mugged getting out of his Mercedes, the car is stolen and he has to get a mini cab all the way back to Devon.

Jan gets back from Tescos with a black eye, plastered with leaflets and won't tell me what happened.

Wife makes shepherd's pie for dinner, really nice! Will look into getting her a cookery show/book deal like Jamie's wife Jools.

Day Four

Great news, Jodie Marsh has said yes to the barbecue! But only if we can get some single blokes to go too. Told Jan, who at fifty-eight is maybe a bit old for Jodie, but as a widower he is technically single so counts towards our quota. He's very keen to meet her and it seemed to cheer him up. He asks whether he still has to wear the cow outfit. Yes he does.

Me and producer go down to the notorious council estate in South London in my Land Rover to meet community leaders and people who live on it. Only five people turn up – Jean, an elderly lady in a wheelchair whose son is in prison. Mike, who claims to have been in the special forces and once went out with Fatima Whitbread – is wearing camouflage gear and keeps shouting "Bring it on! Bring it on!" so things are looking up, and three girls (who seem a bit mental) who think that it's X Factor. We um and ah about it but in the end we let them sing as it's great telly.

Make a mental note to invite Danii Minogue down for the barbecue then worry that she might not get on with Jodie Marsh.

So it's just Mike whom we jokingly refer to as "The Psychopath" and Disabled Jean who pick up the baton for home-reared livestock. Bit disappointing but to be honest that will cut down our overheads and means a larger slice of the pie for me.

Unfortunately when I come out of the meeting the Land Rover has been torched and I am mugged at knife point as I try to hail a cab. If only these kids could learn to turn their knives on cattle.

Get home and there is a message on my answer machine from Darcus Howe asking what his fee would be should he come to the barbecue.

Very disappointing. Why do people always want money for this sort of thing?

We back and forth a few times but get him down to £250 plus car to and from venue, and he seems happy with that.
Wife does roast pork – lovely!

Day Five

The ox calves have arrived and they look great, if a little frightened, especially as we load them into the lift at the estate. After waiting about ten minutes we realise the lifts are not working and try to herd them up the stairs. Mike gets his pit bull terrier out to help with the herding but scares the young heifers and they stampede along one of the landings, knocking over a young mum with a double buggy. The producer pays her off with some yoghurts and invites to the barbecue. We get the calves back down into the car park, where some hoodies have already surrounded the replacement Land Rover, and arrange for a winch and crane. Darcus Howe phones and asks wether he can bring his wife; we say no as this might put off Jodie Marsh. Jonathan Wilkes has got wind of the barbecue and asks wether he can come as well, no mention of a fee either, so that's a relief.

Packed lunch of moles stuffed with rice and sycamore leaves, bag of monster munch and a Ski yoghurt. Not very nice, if I'm honest!

Crane arrives at the estate and we winch the oxen up to the fourteenth and seventeenth floors, where the team are waiting for them.

Mike has already prepared a sort of dungeon area for his calf, which he nicknames "Fatima Whitbread". Jean has some difficulty with hers, it is rather skittish and knocks over a table of tiny Wade figures then grinds the porcelain into the carpet and defecates all over the Linda Barker sofa. Jean sobs remorselessly and it takes the producer and runner a full fifty minutes to persuade her not to pull out of the scheme. I must admit I did feel a bit sorry for her as we left the flat, the ox tied to the shower rail and Jean's tear-stained face looking at us out of the window.

Make mental note to invite Linda Barker to the barbecue.

Fox kievs for dinner, followed by whole box of After Eight mints, which just about took the taste away.

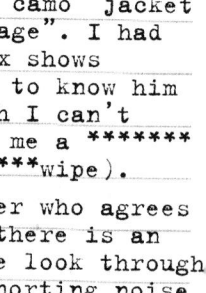

Day Six

Arrive at the estate only to find that Mike has already killed and eaten much of his ox overnight. When I meet up with him he has ox blood all over his camo' jacket and trousers and has smeared ox blood over his face as a "rite of passage". I had explained to him that the idea was to fatten it up over a series of six shows learning techniques of animal husbandry and also the viewers would get to know him and his problems as well but he used a string of expletives at me which I can't reproduce in this diary as I'm hoping for a tie-in book.(OK, he called me a ******* four-eyed dwarf and a ******** straggle-haired **** and a ***kicking, ***wipe).

He asks whether he can have another ox. I discuss this with the producer who agrees on the condition that Mike doesn't kill it without asking us first as there is an overhead involved. Jean meanwhile is not answering the door and when we look through the letterbox all we can see is her legs in the lounge doorway and a snorting noise of the ox coming from the shower room. I suspect she had a busy night and is trying to get some shut-eye.

Meanwhile the crane has been torched and a new one is ordered. Mike's new ox arrives and he binds its feet and carries it across his shoulders up to his dungeon.

Had to skip lunch and just had a Ginsters brunch bar, Kit Kat and a carton of Ribena at Fleet Services on the M3 on the way home.

Day Seven

Arrive at the flats to find the head of Mike's ox impaled on a post outside the main entrance and the words "Four-Eyed Hippy Go Home" written in ox blood on the pavement. This is disappointing. It seems Mike killed his new ox virtually as soon as we left him and when I challenged him about it he took me hostage. I am writing this covertly on my Blackberry. He is keeping me in the toilet and is negotiating with the producer for my release on the condition that he be allowed to rejoin the production with another ox.

The producer texts me to say that Darcus Howe has pulled out. It seems Jamie's people might have got to him. He says he will try and make contact with Jonathan Wilkes's mum to see if he's still available.

Mike gives me raw ox flesh for dinner and a tube of Pringles.

Day Eight

No movement. Still kept hostage by Mike. He shows me videos of Fatima Whitbread from the 1986 European Championships when she broke the world record for a javelin throw. Producer texts me to say not heard anything from our other contestant Jean. Raw ox flesh for lunch and dinner, Chewy bar for pudding.

Day Nine

Mike agrees to let me go if Fatima Whitbread will come to his flat. Producer contacts Fatima's people who know Mike well and refuse to play ball. After a lunch of raw ox liver and Curly Wurly Mike's old sergeant major from the special forces turns up and orders him to let me go. Which he does, sobbing.

Meanwhile Jean seems to have been in the same position in her flat now for the last three days and when we call through the letterbox there is no reply. We batter the door down. The flat is a terrible mess – with much of the furniture broken with hoof marks over it and ox faeces on the floor and some of the walls.

Jean is unconscious, with a hoof imprint on her face and the ox is standing over her, not letting anyone get near.

We get Mike to go in and kill it.

New crane turns up which is then immediately torched by the producer to save time.

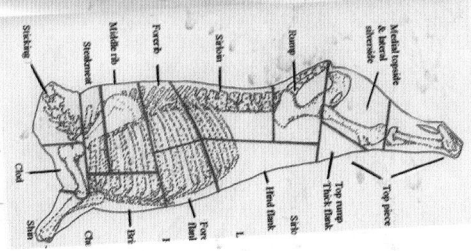

Day Ten

We decide to go ahead with the ox barbecue, although it is a rather subdued affair – just me, the producer, Mike – heavily sedated and handcuffed to a Group 4 guard – and Jean on a drip on a hospital trolley. Halfway through Jonathan Wilkes arrives and tucks into the ox burgers. Nice guy, talks about his close friendship with Robbie Williams and asks where Jodie Marsh is. It seems she has gone to the wrong estate but got lucky anyway and has decided to stay there with her new fellah for a couple of days. The three mental girls from the auditions turn up and ask where Simon Cowell is and when they will hear whether they are going to London. Then they see Wilkesy and he is happy to sign autographs.

As I go to leave, I am jumped by some hoodies and mugged for my shoes, the producer has his Blackberry stolen and his Barbour coat set on fire. When I get home I find that River Cottage has been razed to the ground by one of Jamie's henchmen.

Conclusion

I think we were just unlucky and am convinced that this project could work given proper funding.

Q DID YOU SEE CASUALTY LAST WEEK?
(Mrs B Gilhooley, Epsom)
Yes I did.

Q DID YOU SEE HEARTBEAT ON SUNDAY?
(Mr J Burnside, Manchester)
No, it's been cancelled.

Q DOES HARRY WATCH ALL THE TV HIMSELF OR IS THERE A TEAM OF RESEARCHERS DOING IT FOR HIM?
(Mr D Maier, Tyne & Wear)
Harry currently has a team of 14,000 researchers watching TV for the show; this is a fundamental stage of TV Burp - the watching of the TV. They are based in India in huge warehouses - or "Watching Centres" which from the outside resemble a big B&Q like you'd get on a ring road but insidethe space is divided up into tiny cubicles - just big enough for an armchair, remote control and a TV.

I sit in the main control centre at TV Burp HQ. As our Asian colleagues notice humorous happenings on their TVs they pull a piece of string which runs from New Delhi, over the Himalayas, to a pulley wheel at the bottom of Portugal and thence under the sea to Calais where another pulley wheel directs the string under the English Channel and to London where it connects to a bell. When a designated bell rings, I phone the foreign researcher, (reverse charges call, thus getting the benefits of the low Indian rupee). All conversations are conducted in Hindi to prevent rival shows like Charlie Brooker's Screenwipe, Jimmy Carr's Comercial Breakdown or Lark Rise to Candleford from intercepting our ideas and swiping our gags.

A lady in a chair transcribes the Hindi into rough Estuary English which is then fed to a machine which turns it into typing. Harry then receives the transcripts via fax at his Executive Suite at the Travelodge, High Wycombe and adds them to the script. Because neither of us has ever actually seen the clip we never know if it is going to be funny until the day of the recording and if it isn't funny I order that a laugh should be added, which it is, thus rendering it funny.

Q HOW ACTUALLY FUNNY IS HARRY AND HOW MUCH IS HIS FUNNINESS DUE TO THE FUNNY SCRIPT THAT HE WRITES?
(Mr S Fry, London W1)
You've put your finger on it, well done! It's a well-kept show-biz secret that Harry in private is not at all funny - in fact he has never made me laugh once in all the time that I have known him! He tends to communicate in low whispers and grunts, never looks any of the staff in the eye and is so shy and withdrawn that he insists on attending meetings behind a two-way mirror! If it weren't for the funny script that he writes he wouldn't be at all funny on the show either.

Q DO THE WEEKLY FIGHTS CONTINUE DURING THE COMERCIAL BREAK?
(Mrs A Gillot, Devon)
Yes they do (see centre pages for results). The fights continue until one or other of the contenders is knocked out resulting in permanent brain damage, submit or very rarely is killed. We allow only ten seconds to clear up the debris and bloodstains before part two starts up again which is why we very rarely show the whole studio in part two, particularly if the fight has been messy.

arry!

TV BURP STAR HARRY HILL ANSWERS YOUR COMMONLY ASKED QUESTIONS REGARDING TV BURP...

Q WHY DO SOME PEOPLE SHOUT "FIGHT!" BEFORE HARRY SAYS THE WORD FIGHT, BEFORE THE WEEKLY FIGHT?
(Mr J Clements, London SE12)

You must remember that it is extremely exciting being in the audience of TV Burp, knowing that the fight is about to take place and that Harry is about to shout "Fight!". Often shouting "Fight!" prematurely is a perfectly normal response to this excitement. If however it is becoming a problem and interfering with your enjoyment then it is something that your partner can help you with by staging a fight in the privacy of your own home, but at the moment when she would normally shout "Fight!" she changes the subject and perhaps talks about something non-fight-related such as the pros and cons of a third runway at Heathrow.

Gradually you will find that you will be able to go for longer periods without saying the word "Fight!" until you and your wife say the word "Fight!" together.

Q HOW CAN I GET TO BE IN THE AUDIENCE FOR A TV BURP RECORDING?
(Mr D Quantick, Devon)

People are selected to be in the audience for TV Burp, you can't just turn up and get in. You might be spotted laughing at a live comedy show, such as with the Pub Landlord Al Murray or just laughing at a private joke in the street with a friend. You will then be asked to submit to a lie detector test during which you will be shown segments from TV Burp to ascertain whether you really found it funny or whether you were laughing to just get in on the Zeitgeist Saturday-evening multi-award-winning clip show that everyone is watching unless they're watching Robin Hood or Merlin.

Alternatively you can put your name and address forward and at some point a representative from ITV will stand outside your house during a TV Burp broadcast and rate the amount of laughing you do. If the laughing reaches the levels we require or it is a particularly interesting laugh or one that we've never had before we will approach you to be in the audience for the Ant and Dec vehicle The Saturday Night Take-Your-Money-Off-You show. If you perform well on that and you pass the lie detector test, you then work your way up through Family Fortunes to You've Been Framed, finally to TV Burp. You will be closely monitored during the first TV Burp recording and should your laugh fit you will be fitted with a laminated pass and lanyard entitling you to weekly tickets and a free sausage with every other recording.

Q HOW COME TV BURP KEEPS WINNING BAFTAS AND OTHER TOP-END AWARDS WHEN IT'S JUST A CLIP SHOW AND 90% OF IT IS OTHER PEOPLE'S SHOWS ANYWAY?
(Mr J Ross, Hampstead)

This puzzled us, Jonathan, to be honest! The show is enormously popular with people who make award shows and we think that this might be because it is a clip show – it is easy for them to select a clip from it unlike say a chat show where you have to sit through over an hour of potty-mouthed filth to find something that will run in a Sunday-evening slot and that won't offend the Daily Mail readers. We do have a rule on the show that if any of the shows featured on TV Burp apply they can borrow the trophy. 2009's BAFTA is currently with Jenny Frost from Snog, Marry, Avoid.

Q HOW DOES THE ACTING ON TV BURP GET TO YOU AT HOME?
(Mrs S Shapps, Panama Canal)

1. First the show is recorded in a soundproofed studio on a multi-track tape recorder by SOUND ENGINEERS.
2. This is refined and mixed until it is of a high standard. It is then transferred on to two track stereo tape, with the Dolby button pressed down so it is 'ON'.
3. The tape (a) is fed into a lathe and all the rough edges are removed.
4. The lathed tape (b) is sent by courier and overnight train to Doonray nuclear power station in Scotland. Here the tape is bombarded with atoms until it explodes.
5. The explosive particles fly through the air where they are picked up by your TV aerial or satellite dish if you've gone private.

Q HOW ARE THE TV VIEWING FIGURES WORKED OUT AND WHAT ARE THE VIEWING FIGURES FOR TV BURP?
(Mr D Berg, Spandau Prison, Germany)

Every home in the UK, since 2006, has been fitted with a CCTV camera which is trained on your home's primary TV. Using face recognition software as pioneered on The Bill the mainframe computer can tell which TV personality you are watching and therefore which show – although it has difficulty telling the difference between Susan Boyle and Dr Robert Winston. The ratings for TV Burp have consistently topped 18 million viewers and for that we are eternally thankful to you the great British public – thank you. Sorry no, I got that wrong - that was for Only Fools And Horses, we get about 5 million but thanks anyway.

Q HOW COME THE "TV BURP GOLD" DVD WAS ONLY AN HOUR LONG?
(Mr D Jason & Mr N Lyndhurst, Peckham)

Um, not quite sure, um perhaps we could talk about this at another juncture. Oh dear is that the time I had better get home and er ... Oh look a baby rook! How wonderful.

That's all from me ...

Yours

Harry Hill

Harry Hill

GET RICH

"I MADE A FORTUNE WITH MY AMSTRAD COMPUTER BUT I DOUBLED THAT FORTUNE BY BEING AS CANNY AS A GNAT WITH NO TADGER! THIS IS HOW I DID IT!"

GET RICH
JUST LIKE
Alan Sugar

Here's how to end up as rich as a millionaire! As Sir Alan Sugar shares his business tips from over six years as a top model! *("Shouldn't that be business role model?" – H.)*

HUMBLE BEG-INNINGS

Hello, Sir Alan Sugar here, the famous millionaire off the TV!

Some TV acts can tapdance, sing or tell jokes but not I – no I'm on TV 'cos of me money – nice one!

You've probably seen me driving around in my Rolls Royce along a flyover or maybe overhead in my private jet looking busy as I study my latest business spread sheet. Not bad for a lad who grew up so poor that up until the age of eight I thought that paper money was tiny little paintings that people kept about them for fun! So poor was I that I thought dogs were tiny horses that could be ridden to the fair. So poor, in fact, was I that I thought Terence Trent D'Arby was a river in the Midlands and McFly was a deep-fried insect in a sesame seed bun!

How poor's that for you?!

SUGAR ON MY BUN

So, how did I amass this fortune? Well, I had a brilliant business brain so, unlike some people these days who expect to just go on a TV show and win a hundred grand job at the end of it, at the age of nine, I got off my backside.

Yeah I got off me arse and went down the road to the market and I sold kisses. Yeah fourpence for a smooch, sixpence for a full french snog. With the twelve pence I made off the kisses I bought two dozen bananas, I split them up and sold them for tuppence each – I made forty-eight pence off that little scam, then I followed the people eating the bananas, collected the skins, stuffed the skins with cotton wool, sewed 'em up and sold them on again taking me up to ninety-six pence – almost a pound in today's money. Well, I had to lay low after the banana scam for about a year but while I was in hiding in Scotland I invented the computer – the rest is history. I took a barrow load of Amstrad home computers down London's Petticoat Lane and flogged 'em to the suits on their way home from work. Before I knew it I was filthy rich!

If you want to be a TV millionaire like me just follow my simple top tips

1. Start up a company that sells stuff that everyone wants.

If I had a pound for every time one of me apprentices started up a company selling stuff that NOBODY in their right minds would ever want I'd be a millionaire by now. In fact I am, but that's not the point. I invented computers before anyone had ever heard of the word, but they still knew what one was and that they wanted one. In them days it was different – a computer was the size of a chest freezer and you couldn't play DVDs on them, no, you had to take about half an hour to string up a projector full of film. Backing up your files was a nightmare too: basically you had to be married and get your wife to type everything out using carbon paper in exchange for a bunch of flowers or box of chocs. There was no such thing as the internet neither so you had to actually talk to people, using words. That's where I learnt to say, "You're fired!" And if I had a pound for every time someone came up to me in the street and shouted that at me I'd be a millionaire, which I am, 'cept I don't go out in the street because I prefer to go in me Roller.

2. Check for money down back of sofas.

At the office after you've had a meeting or round at a friend's house when they're in the bog just take the time to stick your hand down the back of a sofa – and see what you can find. Loose change soon adds up.

3. Go metal detecting at weekends.

On the beach after everyone's gone home get down there with your metal detector. People lose all sorts – watches, jewellery and hard cash. Get there early and get out of there early too before they realise what they've lost and come back looking for it.

4. Drink at home, thus avoiding inflated pub prices.

I make up twenty pints of home-brewed beer from kits each month, which works out at about 10p a pint. Easy!

5. Win at raffles at country fairs.

Get down the country fair early and take a look at the colour of the raffle tickets they're flogging. Then get down your local Rymans and buy a matching book of tickets! Better still have a store of all the different-colour raffle ticket books in the back of the Roller. When the time comes for the draw get up the front and claim the prize and skedaddle before the real winner has worked out he's really a loser. In this way I've had jars of chutney, free hair dressing in local salons, free meal for two in a downmarket restaurant or a simple bottle of salad cream.

6. Put old stuff on ebay and get your apprentice to bid for them, thus artificially inflating the price!

7. Replace the powerful 6.75l engine in your Rolls Royce Phantom with a 1.8l engine from a Ford Sierra, and just watch your petrol consumption improve – no one's to know; appearances are everything in business. OK you have to get out and walk up the steep hills but think of the money you're saving.

8. Go on Who Wants To Be A Millionaire on the TV, but dress up as a maintenance man and sneak into Chris's office the night before and photograph the questions with a tiny camera. Then spend the rest of the evening Googling the answers. Put a friend in the audience with the answers on sheets of paper and get them to cough the answers to you – it can't fail. Million-pound magic!

9. Win The Apprentice TV show – like I did in 1954 and I never looked back!

If you're not a millionaire after a year of applying my special money-saving rules write to me and I'll send you a million quid. And if you believe that you're an idiot and YOU'RE FIRED!!!

THE HISTORY OF THE NEWS AT TEN

BY OUR HISTORICAL EXPERT
DR ROBERT SATSUMA

Dah Dah-Dah Daaah !
Da da da-daaaah!
Da-da
Da-da
Bong!
We've all heard it so many times,
the theme tune to The News At Ten, but how
did The News At Ten actually come about?
Let's find out!

PREHISTORIC

Before man walked the earth it was populated by huge lizards like on the ITV programme Primeval. There wasn't anything that we would recognise as news at that time although news was still passed around. For instance if one of the large plant-eating dinosaurs such as a Brontosaurus died and another flesh-eating dinosaur such as the Tyrannosaurus Rex started eating it the smell of the flesh and blood would travel through the air to other flesh-eating dinosaurs who would then come to investigate. In this way the smell is like the news and the T Rex is like a reporter such as News At Ten science expert Lawrence McGinty.

STONE AGE

Once man arrived, things changed very rapidly. Remember man was not how he looks now – no, the metrosexual with emollient facescrub, designer stubble and handbag came much, much later. No, man at that time was much more like one of the people you see on Big Brother. Even though we were just grunting hairy creatures we needed The News. How did it work? Well no one is really sure but from cave paintings it seems that if someone heard a bit of news they would do these cave paintings - quite literally paintings in caves - and point to them and make a series of grunts to add emphasis. A bit like Trevor McDonald does on The News At Ten with his computer graphic illustrations of current events.

ESUS'S TIME

n many ways Jesus was the first proper newsreader. Just like Sir Trevor McDonald he would stand not behind a desk ut on a mountain so that he was the centre of attention and tell the news. In fact he even called it The Good News. nd Jesus took his "Good News Show" all around the Middle East, much as Al Jazeera does now. Sometimes to speed p the news process he would take a donkey. He had twelve other reporters working for him whom he called his sciples. Also he hung out with Mary Magdalene - so it was probably a bit like how Eamonn Holmes and Anthea Turner sed to work together on GMTV – he does one story, she does another and sometimes they share alternate lines. adly Jesus made the news himself when he was betrayed by one of his correspondents and crucified. Fortunately s remaining reporters filed copy and the result is The Bible. Which still makes the news to this very day.

MIDDLE AGES

In the Middle Ages if something happened that was deemed newsworthy a man would run about shouting it out. This man was known as the town crier. To do the job he needed to have a very loud voice.

To grab people's attention the crier would ring a bell before the shouting started up, then he would shout a shortened version of what was in the main bit he was going to shout. This is how what we know as headlines were born. Similarly he would stop in the middle of the shouting for a biscuit and cup of mead. Before this short snack the town crier would let people know that the shouting wasn't over yet and tell them a bit about what he was going to shout about in the next bit. Over the years this became the "Coming Up in Part Two segment" that Sir Trevor McDonald does even to this day. As everyone was listening at this point, local market traders would start shouting in an attempt to sell their wares. Things like fish and meat and also slaves. This gradually evolved into what we know as the advert break where to this day we are told about various items that are for sale such as Tresemme Pure and Simple hair shampoo, Sainsburys Taste the Difference,and Saniflow toilets.

The town crier would finish if he could on an item which was mildly humorous or heart-warming. So for instance he might start shouting about a cat that had fallen off a log into the water trough but had been fished out by a local parson and was fine or maybe about the local fool who thought he was being cuckolded but in fact had got his wife mixed up with her sister. Then another man would shout on about what he thought the weather was going to be like.

In the beginning the shouting was done exclusively by men, but after a while some of the local womenfolk wanted to have a go and this was very popular until the women got older and their voices started to crack a bit and sound a bit witchy. To this day women newsreaders are forced to retire before their male counterparts as it is thought older women will bring bad luck to the programme.

After a while someone had the idea that instead of ringing a bell to tell people that the shouting was starting up maybe they should engage some minstrels to play a short, but recognisable tune. This developed into the characteristic dah dah-dah daahh! theme tune of The News At Ten.

STEAM AGE

This town crier method of spreading The News At Ten lasted for many hundreds of years but because it took so long for the news to reach the town criers in the first place the news was stale and if we're honest wasn't actually news at all but history! So the race was on to find a way of getting the news out faster.

One day James Watt up in Scotland spotted some smoke coming out of a kettle and called it steam. Using this steam he managed to invent the steam-powered train, which could carry news much faster than a donkey or horse. The giant steam train would pull out of Edinburgh station and a Scotsman in national dress mounted on top of the engine would shout the news through a metal cone.

Before they knew it everyone was talking about what was in the new steam news! So much so that even Queen Victoria summoned Mr Watt to Buckingham Palace for a special audience. Imagine the excitement as he sat upon a specially adapted small-gauge steam train that ran around the main drawing room of Buckingham Palace shouting the news as he went. All was going well until the young James Watt incorporated a story about her into his bulletin – about how one of her corgis had fouled in the main throne room. Her Majesty took offence and immediately barked, "We are not the news!" which was misheard as "We are not amused" and entered the history books.

Overall Queen Victoria was much impressed with this steam-driven news but felt that something was missing. She immediately called in her chief architect Augustus Pugin and ordered him to build a giant tower that would house a bell that would go "Bong!" between the various headlines at the top of the show. Thus, in 1858 Big Ben was completed and Sir Trevor McDonald's Bongs! were in place.

RADIO DAYS

In 1896 Guglielmo Marconi invented the radio , but sadly when he turned it on there were no channels, so straight away he set about inventing stations like Radio Italy, Rome 95.8 and Virgin Mary FM. Along with all the top hits of the day such as Just One Cornetto and the theme from The Apprentice the young Marconi realised that this would be the perfect medium to broadcast the ten o'clock news! Thus it was that in 1918 Radio Italy broadcast the first ever ten o'clock news that didn't require someone shouting. Soon everyone was tuned in, even in Scotland where a young wire-haired inventor by the name of John Logie Baird was working on his own invention – television.

TELLY

John Logie Baird was a Scot and could remember quite clearly standing on the corner of Sauchihall street in Glasgow with his mother as the ten o'clock news steam train went by. He would cup his hand to one ear to try and catch the details of who'd won the war or the football results.

One evening on the way home from a ten o'clock news session he passed by a Punch and Judy show and slowly an idea dawned on him. If only it were possible to combine the visual excitement of a puppet show with the factual content of the steam news. He immediately discharged himself from mental hospital and started work in his shed. A year and sixteen days later he emerged carrying a wooden box with a window in it. Placing his gloved hand up inside it and struggling not to move his mouth the puppet appeared to say, "Hello and welcome to the ten o'clock news!" He'd done it! He'd invented televisual puppetry! Straight away he enlisted every Punch and Judy man in the country, thousands of puppeteers were trained – the aim being that there would be enough for one in every house! At ten o'clock every evening the puppeteer would knock at the door, set up his portable booth and quite literally do the ten o'clock news in your front room. Many to this day have fond memories of "Uncle Bob" or "Uncle Paddy" the puppet news anchorman who came to call. Indeed many are the result of couplings between their mother and these Puppet Uncles, who might stay the night too.

But what of Logie Baird himself? No such luck I'm afraid, but he did go on to invent the cathode ray tube and with it what we call the modern telly box.

MODERN NEWS

With so many channels now pumping out news and with the advent of 24-hour rolling news channels like BBC24, Sky News and CBEEBIES, producing ITV's hit show The News At Ten has never been easier. Basically a team of researchers watch the lunchtime news and copy out all the stories, then add the stories from the six o'clock news, then all they have to do is add any stories that happen between 6.30 and about ten o'clock!

NAME THAT SHOW

> SOMETIMES IT CAN BE HARD TO TELL SHOWS APART! I FOR ONE HAVE NO IDEA WHAT THE DIFFERENCE BETWEEN HOLBY CITY AND CASUALTY IS! SO WHY NOT TAKE MY SPECIAL TV QUIZ – AND MATCH THE PLOT TO THE SHOW!

1 PC Wensley's lost his bike. Meanwhile a 1960s stranger causes trouble at the local pub as Buddy Holly sings "Raining in My Heart".
Is it: **a) Homicide: Life On The Street b) The Wire c) Heartbeat?**

2 A skinhead slips on a discarded grape, falling into an old lady on an electric mobility scooter which careers out of control and runs over a child who is already sick with malaria. Meanwhile the nurses are planning yet another retirement party for Charlie. And Kelsey is having a go at computer dating.
Is it: **a) House b) ER c) Casualty?**

3 A train crash in a West Country town, not dissimilar to Bristol, enables a murderer to escape and hide out in a hospital. Meanwhile Nigel from EastEnders is having difficulty hiding his dog from the hospital inspectors and Mr Griffin has become an ebay addict.
Is it: **a) Holby City b) Holby Blue c) Casualty?**

4 A nice woman complains of a tummy ache. Later she dies but not before admitting she could have been nicer to her husband.
Is it: **a) Doctors b) The Royal c) The South Bank Show?**

5 Someone who was hugely famous in the 1970s but is now quite old turns up, playing a rich person who everyone fancies.
Is it: **a) Emmerdale b) Coronation Street c) EastEnders?**

6 Someone who used to be a criminal in EastEnders makes a well-publicised appearance, only this time they're not a criminal.
Is it: **a) The Bill b) EastEnders c) The Six Million Dollar Woman?**

7 A sexy young surfer moves into town and pretty soon all the girls are in love with him – but the guys are teed off! Also a dog is missing.
Is it: **a) Neighbours b) Home And Away c) Party Political Broadcast on behalf of The Liberal Democrat Party?**

8 A woman in a bonnet meets a man in shoes with buckles on. They have a big row and she hates him, but later on she changes her mind and they get married. At some point there is some dancing.
Is it: **a) Cranford b) Lark Rise to Candleford c) Lark Rise to Cranford?**

9 A modern person goes back in time. The haircuts and clothes are different and so are the sweets, also the words used to describe ethnic minorities and women – with funny and often moving consequences.
Is it: **a) Life On Mars b) Lost In Austen c) Cash In The Attic?**

10 A modern person goes back in time – and it's not as good as the first time they did it.
Is it: **a) Ashes To Ashes b) Ashes To Ashes c) Ashes To Ashes?**

ANSWERS

1. c) Heartbeat. Nice easy one to start with. Unless you were nervous, and made a right mess of it.

2. c) Casualty. Charlie's only ever been in Casualty.

3. Not sure. Your guess is as good as mine, frankly.

4. b) The Royal. Because nobody gets ill unless they've done something a bit bad.

5. a) Emmerdale. They specialise in eye candy (even if the eye has a cataract in it).

6. b) EastEnders. It's the law.

7. c) Party Political Broadcast on behalf of The Liberal Democrat Party – they've got a real chance in this next election, I think.

8. a), b) & c) All of them. More please BBC!

9. c) Cash In The Attic.

10. a), b), & c) Well, it was rubbish.

Although he is in The Long Good Friday, where he gets to kiss Helen Mirren.

Springwatch

DOG SPECIAL

Well Spring is here again!

Shut up Kate! Spring is nearly here again and this year we're concentrating on Britain's many dogs.

Shut up I said! Or I'll crush you like a beetle. This year we're concentrating solely on dogs. Look! There's one, quiet! Nobody make a sound! Ouch! It's bit me! Get off!

No it isn't Bill! Anyway, I thought you were leaving!

I don't think that's right Bill.

TYPES OF DOG

DACHSHUND

Known as the sausage dog because of their taste when fried, these tiny, sleek black and brown critters were originally bred to ride Slinkys down stairs at fairgrounds and circuses. Fortunately the practice of the sausage-dog-Slinky was banned by Princess Anne in 1986 so these days the dogs are purely decorative. Prone to problems with their backs they should be discouraged from heavy lifting and are best employing a "man and van" when moving house. They live off marshmallows and Cadbury's fruit'n'nut bars and have been known to catch and kill puppets in the wild such as at a Punch and Judy kiosk on a beach.

Dachshund

ALSATIAN

Although originally from the Alsace region of France many of them these days are third generation and consider themselves British. They have large teeth and claws which can be used for tuning a video recorder or piano. Alsatians love men and many have jobs at the airport or work for the police force although very few of them are self-employed. Although the closest domestic relation to the wolf they have no idea of time and are often late for

Alsatian

meetings, hence they tend to stay at the menial job stage, never progressing through to management.

CHIHUAHUA

These tiny dogs are the result of a cross breed with a mouse and thus love cheese in all its forms except Primula. Their small stature means that they would probably lose if they were ever in a fight with a frog and marmosets have been known to take them on dates if their own date is late. Their tiny hands make them ideal for assembling electronic goods such as iPods or Walkie-Talkies and their high IQ places them in the top three in interspecies Mastermind.

Chihuahua

WEIMARANER

Meaning literally "Grey dog" this dog hails from Germany and was so popular (or pup-ular!!!) between the years 1919 and 1933 that Germany renamed itself after it – The Weimarana Republic. However the rise of Adolf Hitler soon put paid to that and many Weimaranas were forced to act as handservants to Hitler's favourite species – the Poodle. *(SEE POODLE)*

Weimaraner

POODLE

Introduced to France by Hitler in 1942, the Poodle appears on the back of the French flag. Hitler had a crack squad of specially bred blonde-haired, blue-eyed Poodles – all with swastikas shaved into their fur. It was his belief that one of his so-called Aryan Poodles would win Crufts when it was staged in Berlin in 1939. Imagine his disgust when it was in fact won by a Black Labrador called Hymie.

Poodle

FOX TERRIER
Bred to terrorise foxes, these bearded dogs with bushy eyebrows were bred by communists to look a bit like Karl Marx. During the height of the fox invasion of 1923–6

Fox Terrier

a further breed was introduced: the Fox Suicide Terrier would run after a fox, chase it down its hole and then explode. This breed needed careful handling and has all but died out in the UK. Fiercely loyal, these days you only really see Fox Terriers outside the high court when Otis Ferry is being charged for some fox-related affray.

Karl Marx: Fox Terrier

TAPIR
Although not traditionally considered a breed of dog it looks enough like one as far as I'm concerned to qualify. With its long snout, heavyset body and trumpeting bark the Tapir is an excellent companion at something like a rock concert or Glyndebourne Opera festival.

Tapir

They love Indie rock (but not the Kaiser Chiefs) and Wagner (but not Siegfried) but are unreliable pic-nickers due to their voracious appetite for wicker. Tapirs can't swim so don't throw a stick for one into a pond because they'll drown and you'll have a lot of explaining to do to the park keeper as he attempts to drag a twitching South American half elephant from the boating lake as all the children cry, their parents shielding their eyes from this hideous sight.

THE PARTRIDGE
The Partridge is not a dog at all and has no place in a rundown of different dog breeds.

Partridge

With its short, thick beak and beady eyes this colourful game bird made its money from an American television sitcom about a widowed mother and her five children who embarked on a music career. Although initially offered a fee the Partridge held out for a percentage of all merchandise and is thus minted.

PREDATORS
The natural predator of the dog is the goat, which eats dogs. For this reason it is best to keep dogs and goats separate and not take dogs to these "City Zoos" that you see advertised or indeed to Goat World

off the A308, Hampton Court turnoff. The only known antidote to a goat is a cow which will eat one.

Goat: The natural predator

HELPING NATURE
Turn your school into a dog wildlife park by placing bones and bits of meat around your garden. This will encourage dogs to come into the garden. Leave a big pile of old blankets and duvets which the dogs if you're lucky will use to make their nests. Plant posts in the garden which the dogs like to use to pass urine against, but be careful not to get any of their dottings into your eyes, or worse, your packed lunch.

I hope this quick guide to country life has been useful. That's all from me, Bill Oddie, until next time – goodbye!

Help! Help!
He's got me in a vicelike grip! Agh! Stop it!

TV STAR CROSSWORD

ACROSS
1. Amanda Holden was certainly Wild At (5, 8, 2, 3, 5, 4, 3, 7)
8. Jeremy Paxman did this into his hanky on Who Do You Think You Are? (4, 1, 5)
9. Billy Connolly's last series - Journey To The Edge Of (2, 6)
11. What Alan Sugar like to say: "You're...." (2, 4)
13. Chris Moyles climbed this for Comic Relief (1, 5)
17. What Fern Britton put a band round to help her lose weight (3, 6)
18. The Popular American import - Desperate .... (9)
19. Terry Wogan raises money for this every year (7, 2, 5)
21. David Beckham has one of these at the base of his spine saying "Romeo" (4, 5)
22. Paul Potts turned his .... around after his appearance on Britain's Got Talent (5)
26. What Billy Piper likes to do at weekends (3, 7)
30. You've seen it on Dr Who and it's bigger on the inside than it appears on the outside (4, 10, 5)
31. Colleen Nolan twirled around lifting her legs in turn to try to win this (1, 4)
34. Kirsty and Phil's golden rule - Location, Location, ... (8)
35. Callum Best did without it for a month for a TV show (6)
37. Madonna tried to adopt one (7, 6)
38. Heartbeat why do you .... when my baby kisses me? (3, 9)
39. C4's Kevin McCloud has a Grand .... (2, 3, 4)
40. Lark Rise To .... ford (4)
42. What's black, goes round and round and grips the road very well until it eventually goes bald (7, 6, 8, 7)
44. You kiss under this at Christmas (6, 4, 4)
46. What Eamonn Holmes appears on (3, 4, 2, 5, 5)
47. Lift my top up and press my buttons to talk to a friend (6)
48. Creeps over things spreading its tendrils. Holly and the .... (7, 9)

DOWN
1. What Gordon Ramsey likes to put between two buns (4, 8)
2. What Elton and David have once a year to raise money for charity (4)
3. Learn the tricks the conmen use to rip you off on this TV show (3, 3, 4, 8, 5, 8)
4. They tried to make her go to Rehab, but she said .... (2, 2, 2)
5. Barbara Windsor is famous for her .... pinging off into a man's face in a show (3)
6. The part Lee Mead won on You Could Be Joseph (6, 3, 8)
7. From 1667 this man kept a diary charting the day to day goings on in London (4, 8)
10. This larger than life character was a big hit on The X Factor (6, 6, 6)
12. Richard Hammond and Amanda Byram present this assault course challenge contest, Total .... (5, 2, 4)
14. Darren Day says a bird in the hand is worth .... (8)
15. Angelina Jolie and Brad Pitt, and Madonna and Guy Ritchie have both got one of these on a trip to Africa (5, 5)
16. Who was Dion's classic hit 'The Wanderer' based on? .... (7, 5)
20. Susan Boyle made this famous on Britain's Got Talent (3, 9, 2, 4)
23. Jeremy Clarkson presents Top .... (4, 6, 4, 6)
24. Rearrange Piems Rorgan to get this brilliant chat show host (7, 9)
25. Channel 4 ask you to Come Dine With .... (6, 3, 4, 4)
27. In EastEnders Grant and Phil Mitchell are .... (6)
28. With his rod and line Chris Tarrant likes to do this (3, 1, 6, 5)
29. You can get a great feast from Heston .... (8, 7)
32. How much is that Doggie in .... (6, 5, 3)
33. I've got a clever invention which I think I might take to Theo Paphides in the .... (5, 6)
36. Take shelter under Rhianna's .... (9, 5)
41. Snog, Marry .... (6)
43. Children get excited when you mention Chris .... (5)
45. Goldie, Prince and Beethoven are all what? (4)

WHERE'S HARRY?

Can you spot your favourite TV personality amongst this crowd of normal people?

Answer at back of book

For over a decade the X-Factor has provided the music business with valuable lifeblood of much-needed talent. Where once there was a huge lack of young people trying to get on the rock and pop ladder this groundbreaking talent show has thrown the whole music industry a vital lifeline. Ask yourself, where would the world of music be without the likes of Leona Lewis, Alexandra Burke and Scott Bruton *(Not sure who he is – H.)*, three names that have revolutionised the way we listen to and think about music, in their own way as groundbreaking as Mr Jimi Hendrix, the Beatles or Donny Tourette.

The winner leaves the show with a £1m contract with Simon Cowell's label, Syco Entertainment.

Sadly it cannot be that all who pass through those famous X-Factor doors will have a long and fruitful career in the music world *(in fact not even if they win it – H.)* so what of the runners-up, the also-rans and some of the really mental ones?

WHATEVER HAPPENED TO THEM?

TABBY CALLAGHAN

Tabby "The Tabster" Callaghan came third in 2004. The craggy Irish Rock Balladeer still sings in pubs and clubs to fund his "Tabbyworld" project – a theme park just off the Falls Road, Belfast which marries his own idiosyncratic music style with the mating habits of the Tabby cat. "I loved my time on the X-Factor and Sharon was like a mother to me, at least until she lost interest in me," he says.

DANIEL EVANS

Daniel was a runner-up in 2008. This roly-poly uncle type with a penchant for soft rock and who was tipped to go stellar because of his tragic backstory is still singing but only when wearing the heavy synthetic fur suit of Jerusalem the Chipmunk. "I loved my time in the X-Factor and Sharon was like an auntie to me. When things didn't work out in the music biz I had the idea of a rodent that spreads God's word whilst doing walking tours of the Holy Land – hence Jerusalem the Chipmunk was born. Now, although I'm not seeing a penny from my singing, at least God is getting a boost."

RACHEL HYLTON

Rachel came fifth in 2008. At that stage she had five children by five different fathers – the eldest born when she was thirteen, three of them in care – and a history of drug addiction. After some initial interest she found that the only way she could keep in the papers was not through her singing but by having more children – each time with a different father. When she got to eleven children by fourteen different men *(How is that possible? – H.)* she was forced to wear a contraceptive patch by social services. She says: "I loved my time in the X-Factor and Sharon was like an auntie to me. If anyone has seen any of my kids can you tell them that their dinner's ready and it's their favourite – nuggets."

ROWETTA SATCHELL

Rowetta came fourth in 2004 and all looked bright for the former Happy Mondays backing singer. After a recent stint in rehab, she's worked constantly, mainly singing backing vocals for the Happy Mondays – even though the Happy Mondays are no longer around. Many's the lunchtime that you would find Rowetta in a pub with a microphone and amplifier singing Happy Monday backing vocals until someone paid her to stop or broke the microphone underfoot, crushing the plastic outer casing into shards. Sitting at the bar with a broken microphone and some UHU glue she's sanguine about her experience on the pop show. "I loved my time in

the X-Factor and Sharon was like an auntie to me. Can you hold that bit there for me for a moment love – gin and tonic please Doreen and the nice gentleman here is paying."

CHENAI ZINYUKU

Chenai was eliminated in week four of the X-Factor 2005 (week 1 safe, week 2 bottom, week 3 safe, week 4 eliminated). Since then she has had a gap year and then another one and then another gap year which she liked so much she thought she would try and turn Gap Year Pro. Early this year she passed her advanced Gap Year A/S Level and was presented with her certificate by the president of the Gap Year Association – Princess Eugenie.

"I loved my time in the X-Factor and Louis Walsh was like an elderly friend of my parents to me, but I like nothing better than kicking back on a beach in Thailand with a bottle of Hooch and Prince Harry on top of me."

AUSTIN DRAGE
RUNNER-UP 2008

The love child of Rod Hull and his Emu, Austin was shunned for the first eight years of his life for his three-toed feet and long neck which he had surgically corrected by 10 Years Younger surgeon Jan Stanek at his Harley Street clinic and experimentation centre. Throughout this difficult time he cheered himself up by singing.

Drage proved popular with the homosexual community when he pulled up his tail feathers to reveal a bare avian bottom, but sadly this was not enough to get him through to the next round and he was given the order of the boot. Austin spent a brief spell in prison on the Isle of White when he attacked veteran chat show host Michael Parkinson, in a revolving chair.

Mike eventually dropped the charges and they are now firm friends with Mikey often electing to spend an hour on a Sunday rubbing Nivea cream into Austin's avian bottom instead of doing his radio show *(Are you sure about that, it could be libellous – H. This is all totally made up Harry – P)*.

Austin Drage: "I loved my time in the X-Factor and Louis Walsh was like a creepy old neighbour who won't let you walk past the end of his garden to get to the fields behind the house."

THE CONWAY SISTERS

The Conway Sisters (2005). Started life as the Nolan Sisters back in the seventies, and featured Colleen, Denise, Maureen, Bernadette, Beaky, Dopey, Greed and Sloth. When their career started to dip they opted for full body surgery at the Jan Stanek Genetic Modification and Breast Enhancement Centre, in Rye, East Sussex. After a year the swelling had subsided sufficiently for the girls to be relaunched as the Conway Sisters – so called because they believed that what they were doing was lightly, a con. Thought to be the originators of swine flu, they were each stung by a bee which caused their new skin to shrink revealing the original Nolan Sisters only twenty years older, causing them to be ejected from the Apiarist Society's Annual Dinner, where they were doing a lucrative corporate entertainment.

"We loved our time in the hive and were disappointed we didn't get paid in the end but the case rests with the European Court of Human Rights. We intend to spend the money at Mr Stanek's rejuvenation ranch in the West Midlands."

Sixteen-year-old EOGHAN QUIGG

Shaggy-haired, swollen-tongued and with all the gift of the gab you'd expect from an Irish boy, Eoghan (pronounced Eeeeeeooeeeeeeeeooeoeee ogigigigigioeoooeooogggiiggeogggigoigiogghan) Quigg came third in the 2008 finals and was welcomed home with open arms and much cheering and presented with the green velvet robes of the ancient kings of Ireland. After a difficult first album of songs that appealed directly to his fan base – featuring songs such as "I'm The King Of Ireland", "Come, Touch The Hem Of My Green Velvet Robe" and "Brits Out!", Eoghan followed it up with an album of songs mainly about his hair – songs like "Teasy Weasy Cool My Hair Please" and "Gel On My Fingers, Spikes In My Hair". He's now kicked the singing mullarky into touch and is concentrating on a range of hair products and combs.

When cornered outside a salon in Donegal he says: "I loved my time in the X-Factor and Simon was like an auntie to me. Would you like to buy a comb, pal, go on just one, I give all the money to me mammy."

THE UNCONVENTIONALS

A cappella group the Unconventionals comprised Andrew Newey, Drew Jaymson, Elizabeth "Liz" Ewing, Lucy "Loose" Newton, Nicola "Nikki" Dawn and Tom "Mr Thomas" Newman.

The Unconventionals came together just a few months before their appearance on the X-Factor. Drew Jaymson, Tom Newman and Andrew Newey had known each other since 1990 when they both performed at a charity shop at midday in Herne Bay High Street. They followed this up with a gig at the Amusements, finishing with three afternoons at the Crazy Golf. Word soon got round and before they could break up and go back to their day jobs (charity shop worker, amusements bouncer and crazy golf pro, respectively) they were being talked about in Herne as the new "Flying Pickets". Liz Ewing was brought into the group after working with Jaymson on the musical "Crazy G!" a Crazy Golf-themed musical set in Prohibition-torn Ipswich at the turn of the century, where they played boyfriend and girlfriend. Nicola Dawn and Lucy Newton knew Jaymson from the time they all had to share a changing cubicle in Monsoon, during the sales. They were eliminated in the first week.

"We loved our time in the X-Factor and Simon was like a swordfish to us. We would like to have cut his wings off and eaten them with chips but sadly it was not to be."

ANDY ABRAHAM

Fully trained bin man Andy Abraham was a runner-up in 2005. He'd fallen into a wheelie bin the week before the X-Factor auditions and had tried singing a selection of Westlife hits to try and attract attention. He'd been halfway through "You Raise Me Up" when he was literally discovered by one of the show's producers who was out fly tipping and who immediately signed him up for his own wheelie bin. Abrahams played this wheelie bin for a record three months, culminating in one night at the council dump. By now he was covered in household waste and

garden clippings but had made friends with the seagulls, who filled out his application form for the X-Factor.

His first album – "Bin Full O' Songs" – made a respectable 168 in the charts and his second album – "Another Load Of Covers" – failed to chart at all and was sold as a shiny coaster, for drinks *(Yeah I know what a coaster is – H.).*

"I really enjoyed my time on the X-Factor and Simon was like a botoxed-up death's head with luminous teeth to me and I still wake up at night screaming."

STEVE BROOKSTEIN

Steve won the X-Factor in 2004, had a number one single "Against All Odds" and now sits at the very top of the rock tree, rubbing shoulders with rock royalty in his Stella McCartney tracky bottoms, Heather McCartney shoes and Lulu boxer shorts. He regularly hooks up with friends Bono, The Edge and Noel Edmunds but is it all sweet at the apex of the pyramid?

"I loved my time in the X-Factor and Simon was like an auntie to me but anyone who tries to take away my pineapple chunks will be cut down, back off! back off! Back off you midget!" And then he is bundled off by his minders into a red ex-Post Office Transit van.

THE ONES THAT GOT AWAY

LADY GAGA

got through to boot camp in series 3 but was ejected after her Phillips ladyshave failed on the crucial sing-off.

BILL HAYLEY

although knackered from croaking "Rock Around The Clock" for over fifty years made it through to the final nine in series 5. Bill blotted his copy book when he goosed Danii and was out those famous X-Factor doors faster than you can say tetherballs of bougainvillaea.

DIRTY RASCAL

came rapping and jivin' into the audition room like a rocked-out Mr Gadget. Simon, never a fan of the rap genre, just didn't get it. "I don't get it, sorry, it just sounded awful," he said. Two years later he'd changed his name to Dizzie Rascal and was up for the prestigious Mercury Prize. Then took two years off (suspected mercury poisoning).

CHICO

the Moroccan goatherd whose first single, "It's Chico Time", knocked Madonna off the No. 1 slot, was very nearly on the X-Factor but wasn't *(Yes he was – H.).*

SPECIAL REPORT WHERE ARE THEY NOW?

"I thought I told you not to come here!"

"It's got diarrhoea!"

"I see the dog had a nice dinner then!"

"I forced the door so I could take a peek at you in the shower, Luv!"

"I knew I should have kept up the payments, but I couldn't because of the credit crunch!"

"It's times like this that I wish I didn't have to go to work!"

"I hate that food you keep bringing out!"

"I hope it's not a Jeremy Clarkson DVD!"

I feel passionate about the people of this country, especially poor people, and feel constantly let down when I see fat people stuffing their faces with high-fat, unhealthy foods like burgers and chips and pâté de fois gras. Why do poor people buy cheap food and ready meals that are quick and easy to prepare when they could set aside an hour or two every night to cook something out of one of my cookbooks?

I know most murders are committed by someone known to the victim, but where is this nation's sense of friends and family?

I cry real tears of sadness every time I see some down-at-heel dimwit go into a takeaway outlet or restaurant instead of preparing the meal themselves even though I run a restaurant meself (and make a good living at it too!).

I'm absolutely sick to the back of my parrot every time I hear, through a friend, that someone has gone out and bought a ready-made meal from Sainsburys instead of cooking it themselves, even though I do do adverts for Sainsburys, but that's only so I can afford the good things in life, so what's the harm in that?

I feel like bashing me head against a brick wall every time I see some hard-up lardy schmuck actually buying meat and vegetables when they could just as easily grow it on their land like I do, with the help of my head gardener.

Even though I grew up in a pub I feel like topping meself every time I see a bag of crisps go through the till. What a bunch of fat crazy tosspots we in Britain are! I've written to the government but they never seem to do much about it, which is why I'm starting my latest project (with tie-in TV show), which aims to clean up Britain of this foul stain on our national character.

JAMIE'S RULES

Free lettuce for kids: *picture 1*

Kids love lettuce but what are they supposed to do if the schools won't provide it in the quantity they so crave? Many kids are forced to go underground, bringing in their own lettuce, which they grow in the attic in mineral-enriched water and fed by fluorescent lights. Risking a criminal record and high electricity bills and thereby promoting global warming. I say let's have lettuce brought out into the open and distributed to the kids where we can see it. At least then we can wash it, dress it and know that our kids are not inadvertently eating greenfly or maggots.

Free iPod for every kid that eats a carrot: *picture 2*

You can't expect kids to change their diet overnight on willpower alone – you got to have incentives, and as we all know nothing motivates a kid like an iPod. These iPods would be preloaded with my TV series Jamie's School Dinners, which highlighted the problem of dinner ladies trying to get work after I'd virtually killed off the entire school dinner system. Just email in the photos of you eating a carrot as verification and you will be sent an iPod.

Gastric band prize draw: *picture 3*

It worked for Fern Britton and it could work for our kids. I was shocked to discover that many low-income families (poor people) can't afford to have a gastric band done on their kids. How can we expect our kids to get all nice and slim if the health service is letting them down so badly? Combine this fact with the poor person's love of the scratch card and you've got the perfect answer: the gastric band prize draw. Scratch cards, costing a pound each (so it pays for itself), offering the top prize of a gastric band, with runner-up prizes like a carrot or the Jamie Oliver Cookbook.

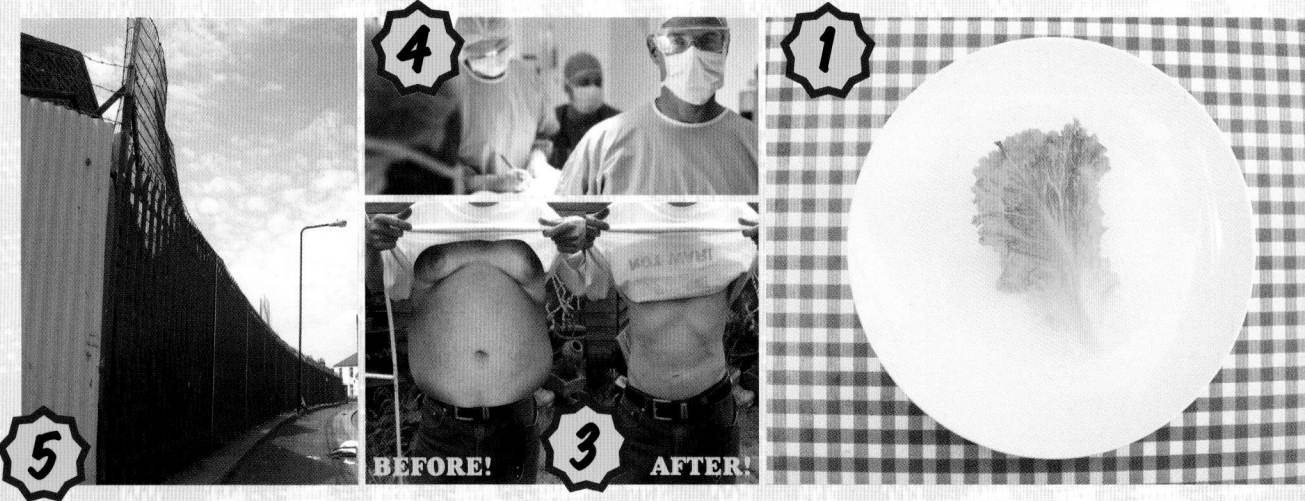

Top plastic surgeon Jan Stanek (off 10 Years Younger) to be made Minister for Health: *picture 4*

I met Jan at Jodie Marsh's bas mitzvah and we got chatting. He has some really interesting ideas about ways in which we can get our young people looking healthier – even if they're not actually healthier. He suggests that all kids, when they hit fourteen, be dragged out into the street and passersby asked to guess how old they are. If their average age is higher than their real age then they are subjected to all measures necessary to get them looking younger – facial surgery, lip injections, teeth enlarging, colonic irrigation and new hairstyle. At first I wasn't sure whether this tall Polish doctor's ideas could work – then I saw 10 Years Younger, and if it works on that, why can't it work for Britain? We plan to pilot the plan in Essex initially then roll it out countrywide the following year.

Metal fence around Glasgow: *picture 5*

With its deep-fried pizza as main course, deep-fried Mars bars pudding followed by deep-fried After Eight mint, Glasgow has long been the capital city of poor diet, heart disease and Aztec Camera. Glasgow constantly brings the health results of the whole nation down. That's why I'm saying let's recognise the problem and contain it. A huge metal Glastonbury-style fence to be erected around Glasgow with regular checkpoints preventing pollsters and health survey experts from entering. Strangers would only be allowed in to film Taggart or Rebus.

Robbie Coltrane to be banned from appearing in films: *picture 6*

What kind of impression does it create to the world at large when one of our biggest stars is not only Scottish but big? Sorry Robbie, I love your work and all that, but sort yourself out or get out.

Kill all firstborn of people who are very fat: *picture 7*

Being fat is probably partly genetic (that's what Jan told me) and in this way we can be sure that we are getting nice slim people who stay slim no matter what they eat and then pass it on to their kids.

Get people smoking again: *picture 8*

Everyone knows you lose weight when you start smoking so let's give out free packets of fags, maybe with an iPod incentive/scratch card promotional offer. The tax we get back off the fags we plough back into the health service, which would then enable low-income families to visit Dr Jan Stanek.

Let's have another world war: *picture 9*

In years gone by there wouldn't be this huge quantity of poor fat people about because they would have been killed in one of the big wars like World War Two. I say let's start a war, let's introduce rationing and let's get the pride back in the national physique. War's good for morale too – unless you're losing. Oddly Winston Churchill was a lot fatter than Adolf Hitler, which is confusing but that may have been because he survived the war by eating huge quantities of whale blubber. We will win through with me, Jamie Oliver, your leader, at the helm.

We're gonna turn this country all lovely slim and healthy – pass it on!

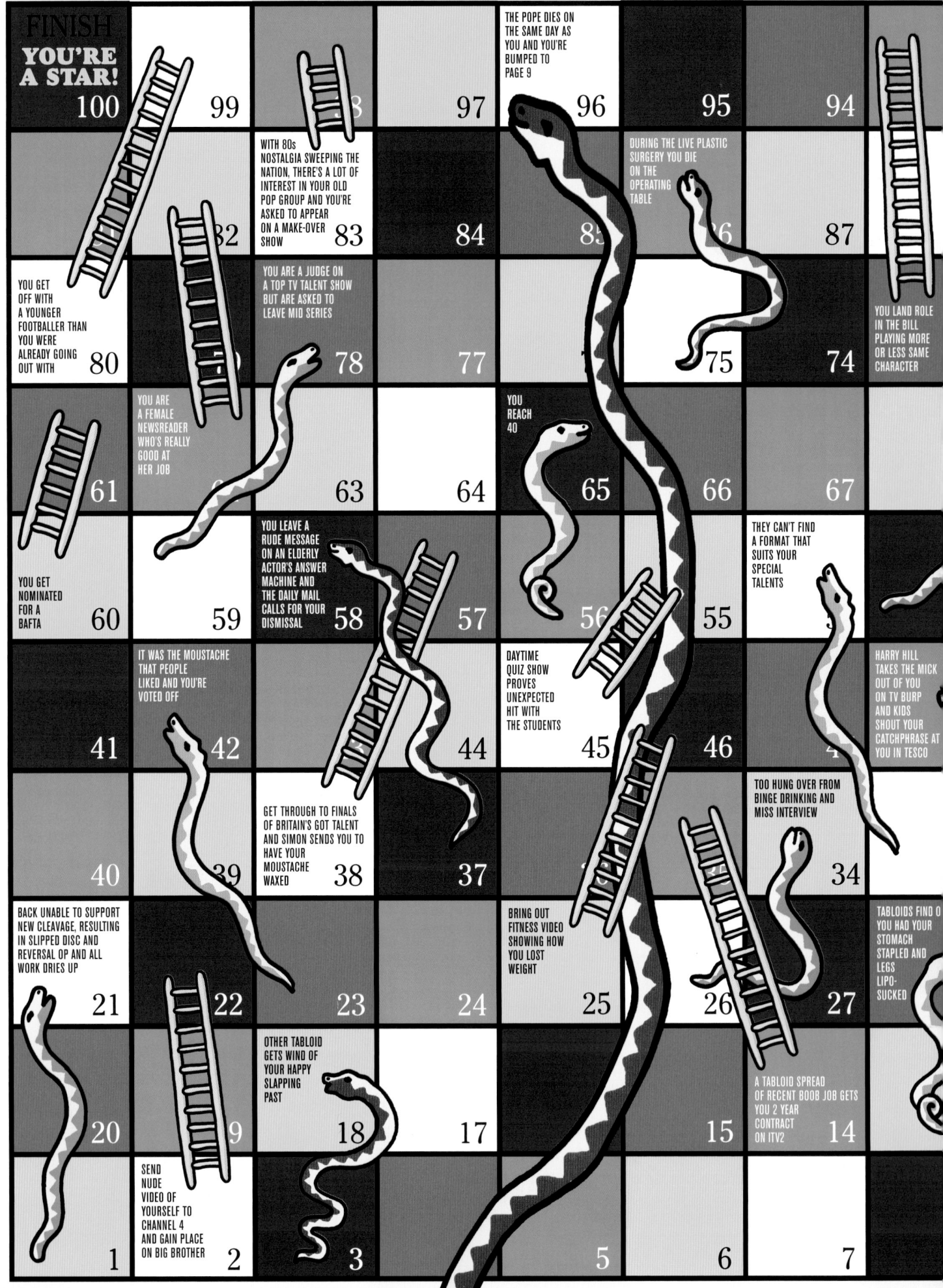

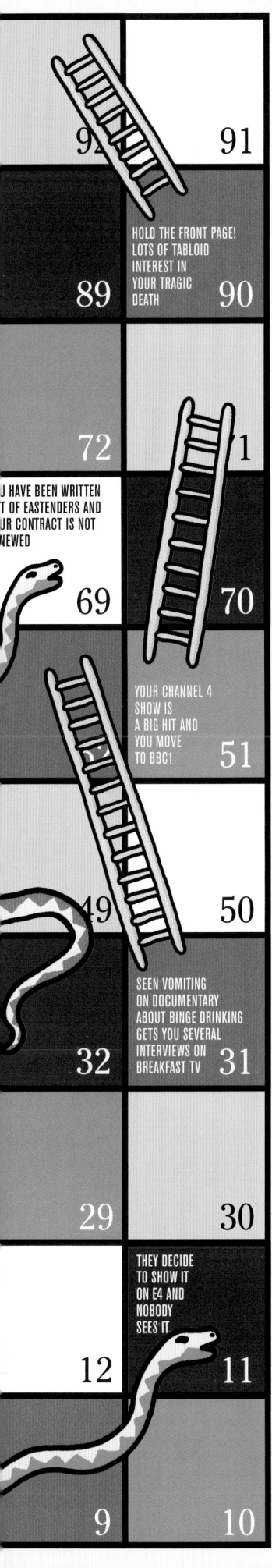

92 | 91

HOLD THE FRONT PAGE! LOTS OF TABLOID INTEREST IN YOUR TRAGIC DEATH

89 | 90

72 | 71

U HAVE BEEN WRITTEN T OF EASTENDERS AND UR CONTRACT IS NOT NEWED

69 | 70

YOUR CHANNEL 4 SHOW IS A BIG HIT AND YOU MOVE TO BBC1

51

49 | 50

SEEN VOMITING ON DOCUMENTARY ABOUT BINGE DRINKING GETS YOU SEVERAL INTERVIEWS ON BREAKFAST TV

32 | 31

29 | 30

THEY DECIDE TO SHOW IT ON E4 AND NOBODY SEES IT

12 | 11

9 | 10

TV
SNAKES
'N'
LADDERS

DO YOU FANCY A CAREER IN TELEVISION?

PLAY THIS GAME AND LEARN HOW IT WORKS

✂ CUT OUT COUNTERS TO PLAY ✂

Rounded Shell Tortoise -V- Tortoise With A Peak To Enable It To Reach Up For Higher Vegetation

Context: David Attenborough's interesting Galapagos Island tortoises on one of his Darwin programmes. A fairly even match, both tortoises being of roughly the same size and weight, so it was always going to be about personality, that fighter's instinct that distinguishes champion from also-ran. As Darwin once said, "It's survival of da biggest" ("I think that should be fittest" – H). Both tortoises entered surprisingly fast considering they are traditionally thought of as slow animals . With adrenaline coarsing through their veins they were galvanised and ready for action. After initial sparring Peak To Enable It To Reach Up For Higher Vegetation tortoise got Round Shell tortoise over on to his back – a vulnerable position for any tortoise.

DURING THE BREAK
It looked to be all over for Rounded Shell but by crossing his back legs he was able to shift his centre of gravity sufficiently to be able to right himself. He then bit Peak To Enable It To Reach Up For Higher Vegetation tortoise on the tail. Peak To Enable It To Reach Up For Higher Vegetation tortoise had already been vulnerable in this area due to a recent foray into some stinging nettles and slammed the floor with his fist in submission. It turns out they're cousins and had previously fought at a wedding. Maybe this gave a psychological advantage to Rounded Shell but you've got to take any advantage you can in a fight.

Undercooked Jacket Potato -V- Cold Bath

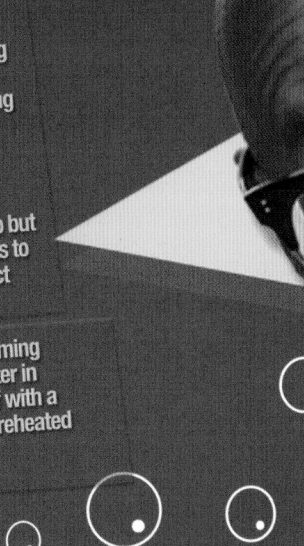

Context: Nigella Lawson compared an undercooked jacket potato to a cold bath. The bath entered gingerly at first and just kind of lay there; in came the jacket potato and fearing a trap hesitated then dived into the bath, kicking its "legs", appearing to be in some kind of trouble.

DURING THE BREAK
The jacket potato's flailings were interpreted by me as showmanship but sadly they were desperate attempts to solicit some help. It could not in fact swim and as its breathing apparatus (a complex series of tubes and capillaries) was submerged in the foaming bathwater it drowned. The message here is that you only need very shallow water in which to drown (although if you're planning to drown someone you're better off with a lot of water as supplied by a lake, or better still, the sea). The jacket potato was reheated and served at the TV Burp after-show party.

Bowl-Headed Girl -V- Cushion-Headed Boy

EastEnders' bowl-headed girl was never the favourite against Coronation Street's cushion-headed boy purely because of gender, but it just goes to show you: never write off the underdog. In she came her slight frame dwarfed by the lanky teenaged cushion head, but with one swift head butt she felled him like a lumberjack at a sapling convention. Then as he lay on the floor in a display that belied her young years, she squashed the stuffing out of his head with her knees.

DURING THE BREAK
This was a real David versus Goliath moment for TV Burp fights and has been cited as the moment there was a big upsurge in interest in the feminist movement. In fact shortly after this ground-breaking fight the female staff on the TV Burp team were given the right to wear trousers at work. On your side, sisters!

King Prawn -v- Baby

Context: An ultrasound of a baby that looked more like a king prawn on Coronation Street. The king prawn came in with an extremely aggressive expression on his face, obviously intended to intimidate his foe. However the baby was having none of it and strode determinedly towards it and slugged it once, twice, three times. The prawn was forced on to its back with the baby on top.

DURING THE BREAK
The prawn wriggled out from under the baby and scuttled off into one corner of the set, behind the sofa. The baby reared up on its hind legs and, frustrated at not being able to see the king prawn started to cry and scream for its mummy.

Its eyesight muddied by tears, it didn't see the king prawn as it sprang from behind the sofa on to the baby's back before giving a huge knockout flick from its tail, propelling the baby into the desk and a full knockout. At this point with the fight over the baby's mum turned up and whacked the king prawn over the head with her handbag before being restrained by studio manager Ray Gearing. The king prawn pressed charges and the mummy was charged with assault. She got a three-month community service order.

FIGHT!

Hitler -v- Heather Mills-McCartney

Context: Hitler and Heather Mills are considered naughty vegetarians on The Restaraunt. Hitler came on all full of himself, like Steve Coogan on a Saturday night. Heather seemed to have an urgency about her that was unbecoming of a Dame. Hitler immediately attacked, as Heather went for his neck.

DURING THE BREAK
Heather was busy strangling Hitler when he suddenly went limp, Heather relaxed her grip, but he'd been faking it, and bought his hand up in a karate chop to the high priestess of Vegetarian Land Mine Charities knocking her back on to the sofa. Suddenly there was a blinding flash and an explosion as a bomb, hidden in a briefcase, exploded, badly injuring Harry. It seems it had been planted by Simon Amstell and his Never Mind The Buzzcocks team in an attempt to usurp Harry in the Comedy Awards. Thus the fight was declared a draw. The perpetrators were rounded up and summarily shot, although before Amstell could be arrested he took a cyanide capsule hidden in his tooth.

Many people write to me asking who won this fight? Or who won that fight? The fact is we never show who wins the TV Burp fights, even though they continue through the advert break until one of the combatants has been knocked out or, rarely, killed. The reasons are twofold – often the fights are extremely gory and violent – especially in the case of a killing, and secondly we do not wish to be seen to endorse one or other of the combatants or violence in general. However with so much time having now elapsed I am able to spill the beans on some of them fights !

Albert the Dog -v- Corky the Parrot

Context: Two new animals on Albert Square. Albert the Boxer Dog had already squared up to Corky in his cage. As the fight was announced Albert came in with his fists up, quite literally in the stance of the boxer. Corky seemed initially confused and clumsy – and looked well above his fighting weight. One blow to the head from Albert and the parrot went down.

DURING THE BREAK
Albert continued to punch Corky repeatedly about the face and beak and it looked like it was all over, then Corky seemed to find some

energy from somewhere, flapped his wings and flew high into the studio ceiling. Corky then proceeded to dive bomb the dog, taking large pecks out of his fur as he attacked. Albert suffered a cut to his forehead, I was forced to step in and call a halt to the fight, declaring Corky the winner.

MiddleEastEnders

middleeastenders

Hey! Did you know that EastEnders has become so popular in the Middle East that they're now making their own version? But with a few changes...

Instead of the Square the Middle East version of EastEnders is set around Albert Oasis – a busy watering hole, and a crossroads for local people. Here we see the Middle Eastern versions of Jack and Max Branning discussing what they're going to do about Tania.

Kath's cafe looks very different on Middle EastEnders. Here we see Ian Beale serving a nice brew to Archie Mitchell (remember they're a bit behind with the plot lines).

Here we see their equivalent of Albert Square Market, but instead of fruit and veg Ian sells large round unleavened breads and giant bananas or plantains. Stacey too has a stall at the market, but far from the raunchy, revealing frocks that her counterpart on Albert Square sells she sells only black full-length burkas – but, of course, they're stolen (which she could have her hand chopped off for under Sharia law)!

Here we see Peggy Mitchell, scouring the Albert Oasis for her sons Grant and Phil.

In Sharia law it is illegal for a woman to run a second-hand car lot and so Ricky Butcher, seen here, is in charge of sales while Pat merely manages the phones.

Pat meanwhile is out shopping for earrings – some things never change!

For religious reasons the Middle East version of Easties cannot be set in a pub. Instead it is set in a pavement cafe. Here we see Charlie Slater relaxing with a hubble-bubble pipe. Don't fancy a fare with him much! If he's not careful he'll be charged with "Being high in charge of a camel" (punishable by death)!

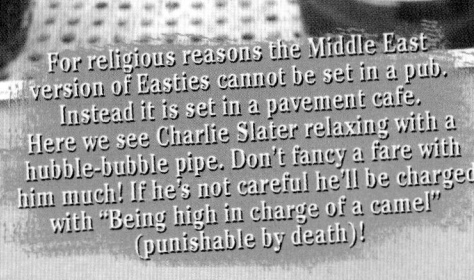

In an odd bit of casting Ken Barlow actor Bill Roach also appears in Middle EastEnders – as the character Mr Ken. He films all his parts in his two-week Easter break from Coronation Street.

THE SIR TREVOR McDONALD STAND-UP COMEDY PAGE

Why are there no dogs at the River Cottage? Because... Hugh Firmly-bit-em-all!!!!!

What do you call the reality TV star who has also won the Grand National? Sir Alan Shergar!!!!!

WHY ARE THERE NO CATS DOWN AT RIVER COTTAGE? BECAUSE OF HUGH'S EARNING KITTEN-STALL!!! (I.E. HE SELLS YOUNG CATS!!!)

Why was Merlin in trouble? Because he developed Arthur-rightus!!!!!

Where does Doctor Who keep his groceries? In the Tardis!!!!!

WHAT DO YOU CALL THE SOAP CHARACTER WHO IS ALSO A PRIVATE DETECTIVE? KEN MARLOWE!!!!!

What is the difference between Damien Hirst's country mansion and John Barrowman's mouth? One has an official arty pile the other an artificial smile!!!

FERN BRITTON HAS REVEALED THAT SHE CAN PLAY THE VIOLIN AND AT THE SAME TIME RECITE THE COMPLETE WORKS OF SHAKESPEARE, WHILST UNICYCLING ON AN ELEPHANT. THERE'S NO DOUBT ABOUT IT, BRITTON'S GOT TALENT!!!!!

What do you call an informal Doctors' dinner party? A Casual tea!!!!!

Which Doctor Who villains always remember to eat their All-Bran? The Fibermen!!!!!

Why are there no gloves down at River Cottage? Because Hugh's a Burning Mitten Fool!!!! (i.e. He burns mittens)

What's the geekiest show on Telly? Eastenders. come on, everyone knows Albert's Square!!!!!

Why is the landlady of the Queen Vic like Shane McGowan's smile? They're both Peggy!!!!

They are doing a crossover episode between Doctor Who and Scooby-Doo. They are calling it Doctor Dooby Doo!!!!!

Why is Phil Mitchell's brother's girlfriend like a posh school? They're both Grant maintained!!!!

BRUCE PARRY HAS SAID HE'S GOING BACK ON THE AMAZON. AND IF HE CAN'T FIND WHAT HE'S AFTER, HE'LL GO BACK ON THE EBAY!!!!!

T. McD. SETLIST
CATS & DOGS (DIFF.)
DRUGS / MUNCHIES
SHARING A FLAT
RELATIONSHIPS/ WIFE BEING A BITCH
FUNNY RAP SONG ABOUT THE WEEK'S NEWS
ENCORE: WAR IN IRAQ.

What patch of water do you go to to gob and pull funny faces in down at River Cottage? No, not the river but Hugh's Gurning Spitting Pool!!!!!

SPENCER'S EMAILS

These are actual emails sent to me during the spring series
of TV Burp by Spencer, our producer.
What kind of job is this for a 45-year-old man? (spencer)
Harry

Tues, Mar 10, 2009 15:18

Subject: TV Burp
Date: Tuesday, March 10, 2009 15:18
From: Spencer Millman
To: Harry Hill

H
After the "the humorous voiceover plays its part" wondered
whether you could do the cat litter swing bin/ fallen over at
wedding and see her knickers joke, cause I like them, they are
funny.
S

Mon, Feb 09, 2009 12:05

Subject: TV Burp
Date: Monday, February 09, 2009 12:05
From: Spencer Millman
To: Harry Hill

H
Please make changes to script attached.
S

STUFF TO PUT IN:

Kilroy snogging the face off his wife
Louis Many Faces – Hitler
Boris – capture Jerusalem
Timmy Mallet touches Joe Swash's mum's knees
Timmy, what am I, who am I?
Emmerdale fire that sounds like a pig – yes it's crackling
Corrie – bone-handle bread knife
Department Store – hair done, nails done, eat chocolate, glass of
champagne and Yo Sushi.

SXX

Fri, Mar 27, 2009 07:00

Subject: TV Burp
Date: Friday, March 27, 2009 07:00
From: Spencer Millman
To: Harry Hill

H,
How's this?
SHAPE * MERGEFORMAT
S

Mon, Apr 16, 2009 13:02

Subject: TV Burp
Date: Monday, April 16, 2009 13:02
From: Spencer Millman
To: Harry Hill

H
I know you will not like this but think we should cut this section
this week. Not because of the Taliban Crossroads but just don't
think the staring clip works or is that funny and think we should
wait until we have more stuff. Think just having the Crossroads
thing by itself is odd. When we have more stuff from Ross then we
can do the Crossroads VT
S

Subject: TV Burp
Date: Tuesday, January 20, 2009 09:23
From: Spencer Millman
To: Harry Hill

H
Have you gone off the boobs look like my bum of the week?
S

Subject: TV Burp
Date: Friday, March 27, 2009 15:20
From: Spencer Millman
To: Harry Hill

H
Who is Dr Gayner?
S

Wed, Jan 14, 2009 16:48

Subject: TV Burp
Date: Wednesday, January 14, 2009 16:48
From: Spencer Millman
To: Harry Hill

H
Also just a quick point, in the changing channel line with the Pig
would it make more sense to try a non-ITV programme?
S

Thu, Jan 22, 2009 08:47

Subject: TV Burp
Date: Thursday, January 22, 2009 08:47
From: Spencer Millman
To: Harry Hill

H
What do you want the mermaid to be wearing on top as normally
they would be naked!?
S

...32

...arch 19, 2009 09:32
From: Spencer Millman
To: Harry Hill

H
Not convinced by the middle leg woman. If you want to do the man
with one leg did you have anyone in mind?
S

Wed, Apr 01, 2009 04:35

Subject: TV Burp
Date: Wednesday, April 01, 2009 04:35
From: Spencer Millman
To: Harry Hill

H
So not sure if you agree but I think the pulling pants down is either
the sketches or Bradley Walsh. What you think?
Also think Paris Hilton boxer shorts rather than pants. Are you
seriously telling me you would be comfortable standing on set on
national television in a pair of Paris Hilton pants!!!
S

Subject: TV Burp
Date: Tuesday, March 10, 2009 19:45
From: Spencer Millman
To: Harry Hill

H
I put back in my bum looks like your boobs, think it's funny unless you are really anti it?
S

Tue, Mar 10, 2009 19:35

Subject: TV Burp
Date: Tuesday, March 3, 2009 05:30
From: Spencer Millman
To: Harry Hill

H
10 years younger is fine now, just waiting to hear back about squirrels
S

PS CUT Turkey has a lie-in on Emmerdale

Subject: TV Burp
Date: Saturday, March 21, 2009 14:16
From: Spencer Millman
To: Harry Hill

H

Have a look at email below, it's long and boring but you should have a look as the whole Bolero thing could be a massive pain for us.
S

Subject: TV Burp
Date: Wednesday, April 2
From: Spencer Millman
To: Harry Hill

H
Lionel Blair?
S

Wed, Apr 29, 2009 23:51

Wed, Mar 25, 2009 15:11

Subject: TV Burp
Date: Wednesday, March 25, 2009 15:11
From: Spencer Millman
To: Harry Hill

H
I like the monkey stuff think it's funny. However I think after the spit out from the yellow bottle move on to Time Team and cut the 2nd Hottest Place on Earth clip. Also don't you need to be drinking from the similar black cup before the VT. The way you have it at the moment doesn't quite work I don't think as why would you drink it having seen her collect pee in it (god I sound like Ronnie Corbett!)
S

Sun, Feb 22, 2009 11:11

Subject: TV Burp
Date: Sunday, February 22, 2009 11:11
From: Spencer Millman
To: Harry Hill

H
Have checked the Emmerdale tapes here in office and all are working fine. Do you want us to buy you a new VHS player?
S

Subject: TV Burp
Date: Thursday, M
From: Spencer Mi
To: Harry Hill

H
John Sergeant is away out of the country until next week so not around to do sketch. Shall we go from woman falling into desk from cracker pull into highlight of the week? Or do you still want to do something with this as a sketch but not with John?
S

Tue, Jan 29, 2009 08:19

Subject: TV Burp
Date: Tuesday, January 29, 2009 08:19
From: Spencer Millman
To: Harry Hill

H
How are you going to liquidise your hands???
How do you see this working live?
S

Fri, Mar

Subject: TV Burp
Date: Friday, March 20, 2009 13:45
From: Spencer Millman
To: Harry Hill

H
Script attached, please make changes to this one.
Ta

things to put in:
mily belly button (opener part 2)
imewatch:
hip called penises (opener part 2)
ARIS:
aby pig
erret in pants
really like pigs
ets' frogs and birds

Thu, Feb 19, 2009 17:17

Subject: TV Burp
Date: Thursday, February 19, 2009 17:17
From: Spencer Millman
To: Harry Hill

H
Please make changes to script attached.

Cut the marmoset boobs. So go from marmoset disappears into "Holly, have you managed..."

Believe that is it. See you later
S

Mon, Jan 12, 2009

Subject: TV Burp
Date: Monday, January 12, 2009 15:11
From: Spencer Millman
To: Harry Hill

H
Just seen my email on your website, very funny.
How mad does it look out of context!
See you in morn
Sx

My Perfect Night In

PETER DOHERTY

Play with Lego.
Write 12 songs.
Do a blood painting.
Pass out..

FIONA BRUCE'S
HILARIOUS ANTIQUES ROADSHOW ANECDOTES
SOME OF THE MADCAP SCENARIOS THAT HAVE TAKEN PLACE ON
BRITAIN'S PREMIER ANTIQUES MONETARY ASSESSMENT SHOW

Hi, I'm Fiona Bruce, what's your problem?
As you can imagine if you get members of the public, antiques and antiques experts together in one room that's a recipe for hilarious anecdotes. I've handpicked some of my favourites.

HILARIOUS ANTIQUES ROADSHOW
ANECDOTE NO. 1
THE SMELLY OLD DOG TOWEL

I remember in Leeds that time, or was it York? I forget exactly. Anyway it was a lot of fun! This woman came in with a painting. It was two metres by one metre and she said it had been given to her by an American gentleman with straw-like white hair who used to live in New York. I said, "What's Mike Aspel doing in New York?" Of course not, I'm kidding! She didn't think it was worth anything – not a bean. In fact she just used it as a towel and not even to dry herself off but to dry her dog!! And it wasn't even a small dog, no it was a massive St Bernard – one of the biggest dogs you can get! Not only that but the pooch's favourite habit was to roll in faeces!! Not just its own faeces either, but foul-smelling fox faeces! Anyway, a neighbour had seen something very similar hanging in the Tate Gallery of London – which only shows the most valuable paintings known to man! She suggested our friend bring it along to The Antiques Roadshow. The lady thought, "What would they want with my old fox faeces ridden oil painting towel that silly Mr Warhol had given me?" Anyway she decided to bring it in but on the day of the show she discovered that she'd been booked in for a hysterectomy – so couldn't make it! So her daughter said she'd bring it along, but on the way she was involved in a massive car accident. She was cut from the wreckage of her Nissan Micra and would you believe it the oil painting was only slightly damaged! The daughter explained to the ambulance driver that she was trying to take the painting in to the Antiques Roadshow with Fiona Bruce and he offered to deliver it for her on the way home from the hospital. Well he just made it through the doors of Leeds town hall (or York) and it was the last antique to be assessed. Art expert Rupert Maas took one look at it and declared it, not an original Andy Warhol painting but a clever fake and worth only about fifteen quid. Not bad for a smelly old dog towel! When we heard the story of how it had got to us everyone collapsed in a big old heap of laughter!

HILARIOUS ANTIQUES ROADSHOW
ANECDOTE NO. 2
THE MYSTERIOUS EASTERN-LOOKING VASE

It was in Llandudno, I think, or Swansea when a lady bought in a mysterious and valuable-looking vase. We asked her the story behind it and she explained that her father had happened upon it at an auction at top antiques dealers Sothebys and had snapped it up for £150,000. The girl, who didn't want to be identified, went on to explain that she was sadly addicted to gambling and so to her the piece was just "some mysterious-looking eastern vase that was worth a bomb which I could cash up and have a big win on the horses and finally turn my life around". Sure enough our expert Bob Smart looked it up on Google and found out it was worth about £150,000. Seeing the girl was desperate he was able to buy it off her for a bargain £3,000. The girl grabbed the cash and was gone. How we all laughed at this wrong-headed loser! Not bad for some old eastern-looking vase.

HILARIOUS ANTIQUES ROADSHOW
ANECDOTE NO. 3
VALUABLE JUNK?

This time we were in Edinburgh, or was it Glasgow, no Edinburgh, I'm quite sure of it. Anyway this odd-looking gentleman approaches Sarah Croker-Poole-Staples, our expert in toys and memorabilia. Dressed in a thick glasses, a long raincoat but no trousers or pants and pushing a wheelie bin full of stuff, he described himself as Ben – a collector. He explained that he'd collected a whole load of back issues of The Sun newspaper dating back to 2006 and collected those plastic discs with photos of the England Team on, from Euro 2004, and also had a huge VHS tape collection of the News at Ten. He said all his family laughed at him and his mum had even once tried to throw the stuff out! Once she succeeded but Ben ran down the road after the bin lorry shouting and crying and got them back although many of the discs were now broken or scuffed. Sarah Croker-Poole-Staples took one look at this Aladdin's cave of stuff, wiped the garbage off them and declared them: "Very interesting, a fascinating insight into someone's descent into mental illness."

Naturally Ben enquired of the value. "To put a price on them, well, they're priceless to you, Ben, " she said, "In fact if someone tried to take them away from you, you would become violent, but thanks for bringing them in, you can stop holding my hand now, ow! Ow! You're hurting me!" In the end she gave him twenty quid and he left. How we all laughed at this funny man! Not bad for a wheelie bin full of junk, eh?!

THE EXPERTS

LIONEL FINLAY-QUAY, 58

Area of expertise – wood. If it's wooden or made of wood he's got an opinion on it. Loathes tables and don't go near him with a laminate.

BUNTY STENT, 51

Area of expertise – soft toys that have been used to smuggle stuff through customs. Favourite item a 1930s Steiff bear that when opened contained a big bag o' gems.

BOB SMART, 35

Area of expertise – china stuff, especially jugs. Son of ex-Antiques Roadshow expert Duncan Smart who gave him the job for his 30th birthday to stop him getting in trouble with the law. Looks just like his dad, only older.

SARAH CROKER-POOLE-STAPLES, 48

Area of expertise – rock and pop memorabilia. Recently managed to verify a turn-up that once adorned the bottom of Buddy Holly's trousers, a half-used box of firelighters used by Jimi Hendrix to set fire to one of his guitars during the harsh winter of 1963 and a rock cake that Bob Monkhouse left on his tray at the Fleet Services, off the M3. She certainly knows her trousers.

GEOFFREY HAYDN-HANDLE, 63

Area of expertise – lolly wrappers from the 1970s. Has the largest collection of lolly wrappers in Europe including a rare 1977 lemonade sparkle where the "e" of sparkle is missed off, and the only Lord Toffingham wrapper in existance (a tongue of soft toffee fudge enrobed in caramel-flavoured ice). Sadly the collection is of superficial interest only and completely worthless.

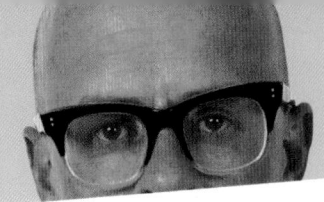

tutwits

Your favourite stars reveal what they're doing – right now!

Home

COLEEN NOLAN :·) Locked in a lab in Shrewsbury with boffins putting the finishing touches to my Loose Women Pelvic Floor Exerciser
2 minutes ago from tv twit feed

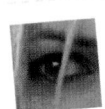
jenni falconer x Is currently destroying a Kenny G 'Best Of' Box Set with a ball-pane hammer.
6 minutes ago from tv twit feed

Frances (secretary in The Apprentice) I'm stuck in a well!
7 minutes ago from tv twit feed

>mark durden-smith< On the final day of a barrel making course in Oswestry.
9 minutes ago from tv twit feed

Beverley Callard Parked outside The Trafford Centre listening to pirate radio whilst working my way through two pounds of haslet.
14 minutes ago from tv twit feed

X FOUR-POOFS-AND-A-PIANO X We're defacing library books in Chalfont St Mary............
17 minutes ago from tv twit feed

Kevin Whately just popping out to buy a spark plug for my ride-on lawnmower.
19 minutes ago from tv twit feed

eoghan_quigg playing call of duty 4: modern warfare for the ps3 on line with sir andrew lloyd-webber.
23 minutes ago from tv twit feed

ainsley harriott Lisa Tarbuck's popped round and we're half way through a Desperate Housewives marathon!
23 minutes ago from tv twit feed

TRINNY_WOODALL HEADING HOME FROM COSTCUTTER WITH 6 CANS OF BUDGET LAGER AND A JAR OF DOLMIO.
25 minutes ago from tv twit feed

dermot o'leary Training my dancing bear, well, bearded Collie.
27 minutes ago from tv twit feed

Harry Hill Just popped open a tin of Sild!
29 minutes ago from tv twit feed

raymears is eating a POT RICE. they're so convenient, aren't they?
3 minutes ago from tv twit feed

ray quinnnnnnn Looking in the mirror – and liking what I'm seeing!
7 minutes ago from tv twit feed

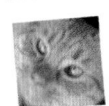
xxFEARNExxCOTTONxx ON MY WAY TO MARKET TO EXCHANGE A COW FOR SOME MAGIC BEANS!
8 minutes ago from tv twit feed

austin healey holding an impromptu seance with bruno tonioli, kate silverton and the cast of we will rock you.
13 minutes ago from tv twit feed

BEAR GRYLLS is SKINNING A VOLE.
17 minutes ago from tv twit feed

Martin Clunes Is making his own fireworks from match heads and lighter fuel.
18 minutes ago from tv twit feed

'Deano' Gaffney In Smiths thumbing through Practical Caravan.
21 minutes ago from tv twit feed

THE BANKER sitting around at home just about to ring Noel.
23 minutes ago from tv twit feed

connie huq torching a friend's car.
24 minutes ago from tv twit feed

Stephen Fry Still stuck in the lift. HELP!!!!!!!!!!!!!!!!!!!!
26 minutes ago from tv twit feed

Michael Parkinson Taking grandchildren to meat processing plant in Preston.
28 minutes ago from tv twit feed

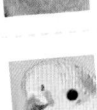
MRS HILL On the Wii Exercise but put off by strong smell of fish.
30 minutes ago from tv twit feed

What Would They Be Watching Had They Lived?

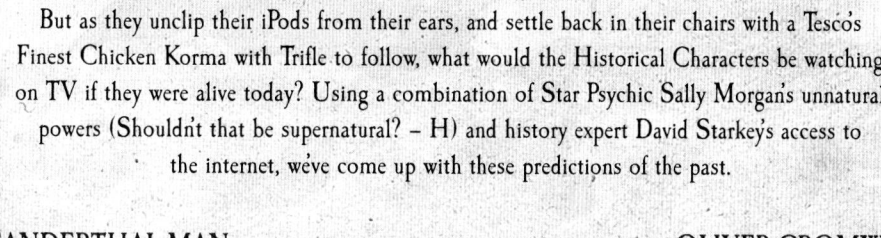

by David Starkey with help from Sally Morgan, Star Psychic

If they had lived some of them would be over a hundred years old!

But as they unclip their iPods from their ears, and settle back in their chairs with a Tesco's Finest Chicken Korma with Trifle to follow, what would the Historical Characters be watching on TV if they were alive today? Using a combination of Star Psychic Sally Morgan's unnatural powers (Shouldn't that be supernatural? – H) and history expert David Starkey's access to the internet, we've come up with these predictions of the past.

NEANDERTHAL MAN
Big Brother

JESUS CHRIST
Xtreme Fishing With Robson Green

PONTIUS PILOT
Gladiators

JUDAS ISCARIOT
Grumpy Old Men

LAZARUS OF BETHANY
Holby City

KING ALFRED
Can't Cook Won't Cook

WILLIAM THE CONQUEROR
Robot Wars

KING HAROLD
Casualty

RICHARD III
Springwatch

RICHARD THE LION HEART
Lion Man

WILLIAM 'BRAVEHEART' WALLACE
Neighbours

ST FRANCIS OF ASSISI
Animal Hospital

GENGHIS KHAN
My Family

THOMAS BECKET
Last Of The Summer Wine

ELIZABETH I
Changing Rooms

MARY QUEEN OF SCOTS
Billy Connolly's Journey To The Edge Of The World

HENRY VIII
Snog, Marry, Avoid

OLIVER CROMWELL
The State Opening Of Parliament

GUY FAWKES
Brainiac

LOUIS XIV THE "SUN KING"
A Place In The Sun

NAPOLEON BONAPARTE
Shipwrecked

JOSÉPHINE DE BEAUHARNAIS
Hollyoaks

WOLFGANG AMADEUS MOZART
Any Dream Will Do

LADY GODIVA
What Not To Wear

ADOLF HITLER
Crufts

WINSTON CHURCHILL
Top Gear

MAHATMA GANDHI
How To Look Good Naked

MICHELANGELO
Skins

GEORGE WASHINGTON
Paris Hilton's British Best Friend

VINCENT VAN GOGH
Art Attack

WILLIAM SHAKESPEARE
EastEnders

CHARLES DICKENS
Coronation Street

OSCAR WILDE
The Eurovision Song Contest

P. T. BARNUM
The X-Factor

If you are the ghost of an historical character and are reading this over the shoulder of a live person then get in touch, we'd love to know what you're watching tonight

It's been a whirlwind romance but to look at them now you'd never guess that they'd only known each other for three weeks. The Knitted Character from EastEnders – or "KC" as he prefers to be known – and Julie Hesmondhalgh who plays transsexual Hayley Cropper on Coronation Street – relax with a Nintendo DS each as their newborn baby Lacey rolls around on the floor at their feet trying to retrieve a wine gum from under the sofa.

"Baby Lacey loves having her picture taken," says Julie. "I don't know where she gets it from!" She laughs and nudges KC, who is annoyed at losing his place on his Super Mario game. "Oi! I was just about to kick a mushroom and get a gold coin, careful Julie!" he says tenderly, snapping shut the device and slinging it across the room. It shatters on the beautiful marble fireplace and one of the batteries falls within easy grasp of the baby, who proceeds to suck it.

Here the couple open up to HELLO! for the first time about their special relationship and their hopes for Baby Lacey.

This is quite a house. Have you lived here long?
KC: "No, we don't really live here, we borrowed it for the shoot off Brian Conley."

Oh. How did you two meet?
J: "We met at the Soap Awards. I was presenting one and KC was up for best stunt in a soap by a person of knitted skin."

KC: "That's right, I was up against Knitted Duck on Hollyoaks and a Teddy on Corrie, but I won it.

It's cool because we're all good friends and had a laugh about it at the bar afterwards, which is where I saw Julie."

Was it Love at First Sight?
J: "Yes."

KC: "No ... I mean yes ... we ..."

J: "He spilt some juice down my cleavage and offered to help me get out of my wet things."

KC: "That's right, and as I was sponging her down she leant in for a kiss and we snogged, didn't we?"

J: "Yes, but I didn't really think anything of it – it was really only when I went round to his place the following week

to retrieve my socks that we got chatting and really got to know each other."

Because you are so different, did you have any opposition from friends or family to your relationship?

J: "There's a lot of prejudice towards Humano–Knitted relations, which is partly why we're doing this interview."

KC: "Your dad was furious, wasn't he?"

J: "Yes, he locked me in my room for a night to try and prevent me from seeing KC and I had to escape through a window and shin down a tree to escape and got a splinter in my bottom."

KC: "I applied ointment to it, which was another sort of bond we have."

J: "Dad soon came round, though."

KC: "I went round and started talking to him through the letterbox, promising him treats and money and that and in the end he opened the door and we went down the pub and now we're the best of friends."

How much did you have to pay him?

KC: "Well, that's the other reason we're doing this interview: to raise money to buy his approval."

Does Dad let you share a bed together when you stay round his place?

J: "Not sure we need to answer that."

Sorry. When did you discover you were pregnant, Julie ?

J: "Pretty much straight away. At first I couldn't understand it because we'd never actually, you know, then KC explained that it's different for Knitted folk."

KC: "Yes, for someone who's Knitted you only have to snog someone for them to get pregnant if there's enough wool about."

J: "The first I knew about it was when my cardigan started to get smaller."

Because you were getting bigger ?

J: "No, the wool was being absorbed by my body to provide for the child. Little Lacey here."

How was the pregnancy? Did you find it easy ?

J: "Not at all! No, I suffered a lot with regurgitation. I would bring up balls of wool in the morning mainly and of course it played havoc with my filming schedule."

Of course, you were still filming Coronation Street at the time.

J: "Yes, so they had to film me from the neck up or I had a body double for nude scenes like the bit when Dev and I, you know, the shower repair scene."

KC: "I don't think that's gone out yet, love."

J: "Oops! I didn't tell you that. You won't print it will you?

No, I'll make sure we cut it out.

J: "Thanks, I could lose my job if …"

How did you break the news to KC?

J: "He found twenty pregnancy test sticks in the bin."

Twenty?

J: "Yes, I wanted to be sure, you know, before telling him."

How did you react when you found out you were going to be a father?

KC: "Bit shocked to be honest"

J: "He got a bit violent."

KC: "Well I don't think there's …"

J: "He broke up a chair and table with an axe."

KC: "A small hatchet actually but it was a spur-of-the-moment thing."

J: "It took him over a week to completely smash them up. Then you came round to the idea."

KC: "Yes, well when Julie explained that you might be interested and how a baby can raise your profile."

Tell us about the birth, Julie.

J: "Pretty straightforward really."

KC: "The gestation time for a Knitted being is only three weeks, so it wasn't a long pregnancy."

J: "No, and to be honest I hardly felt a thing."

Where was Baby Lacey born?

"Heston Services, off the M1, in Burger King. Yes, I'd popped in for a Whoppa and came out with a lot more than I bargained for! Ha ha!"

KC: "Ha ha! Ha Ha ha Ha Hee hee ho ho!"

"He broke up a chair and table with an axe"

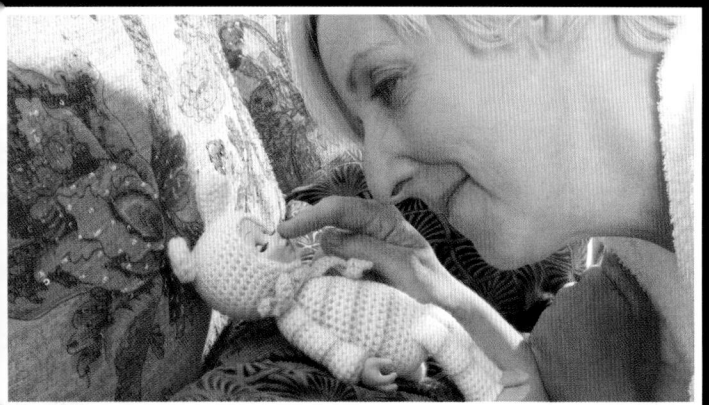

Where were you, KC?

KC: "I was um, it's a bit difficult …"

J: "You might as well tell them. It will come out eventually."

KC: "Listen, I regret it now and me and Julie are cool with it now but …"

J: "He was with another woman."

KC: "With Samantha Janus. We got close during EastEnders filming and Julie hadn't returned any of my calls …"

J: "I'd used up my minutes, I'm pay as you go …"

KC: "So … anyway it's all water under the bridge. We're together now."

Did you have any cravings, Julie?

J: "I craved attention from KC and, to a lesser extent, wool."

Why did you choose the name Lacey? Was it because of your much-publicised friendship with Lacey Turner who plays Stacey Slater on The Square, KC ?

J: "What?!"

KC: "That's all over, no, we called her Lacey because her face is sort of …"

J: "Lacey."

KC: "Yeah, it's the combination of the human and Knitted genes I think."

How is Baby Lacey developing?

J: "Oh she's a joy to be with, I love her little hands and feet and the way she looks at me when I'm handing her over to the nanny."

Should she be that blue colour?

KC: "Eh? Oh flaming Nora! She's choking on that battery, you crazy mare! Quick, get her on her front!"

J: "Don't call me a crazy mare, you jumped-up little ball of yarn!"

KC: "Ouch! Right! take that you …"

At this point the phone rings.

J: "Hello? Who!? It's for you. It's Samantha Janus!"

KC: "Hello Sam, you're what?!!! That's impossible!"

We'll leave it there I think.

KC: "Get lost!"

J: "He doesn't mean it. We'll still get paid, right?

> "I craved attention from KC and, to a lesser extent, wool"

My TV Poems *by* Holly Willoughby

"In my spare time I like to write poems about the top TV shows,
I have chosen three of my strongest poems to share with you and hopefully raise some money for charity"

THE BILL POEM

Da da da daaah da da daaah daaah
Dah da-da da da
Daaaah da-da da dah
Da!

Trouble down The Jasmine Allen Estate!
Shouts Jack Meadows, adding "Don't be late!"
When they get there Terry Stamp and co.
Grab some youths who they thinks might know
Something about a recent affray
Where a young lad was bullied for being gay
Or because he had a limp
"Oi! Pooftah! Hopalong! What a whimp!"
They were heard to shout at the hapless lad
What is it that makes people turn bad?
Is it their upbringing? Nature or nurture?
Whatever it is, they'll try and hurt yer.
Whether with a beating, knife or gun
Or stealing a car that they'll use to run
Over your mum as she comes out of the flats
Knocked down, lying bleeding amongst a heap of rats
No wonder Superintendent John Heaton doesn't give a dime
For those who are touchy feely and soft on crime
John is a man of integrity who will stand by his men
As well as being opinionated and direct, he's a a workaholic, do ya ken?
If he sees someone with drugs, puffing on a roach
He takes a tough, zero tolerance approach
To his mind criminals have been getting away with it for far too long.
So put away your king-sized Rizlas, dope and bong!
You may take the cynical view that Heaton's just asserting his authority
To secure some good arrest statistics and advance his own career
But I'll have no truck with that, get outta here!

In summary then, suffice to say,
It doesn't always go his way.
So if you've got a night in or are in bed ill
You could do a lot worse than watch ITV's The Bill.

HOLLY OAKS

Oh! Holly Oaks
You are my favourite soap folks
I'm hooked, you're booked.
Beautiful Teens
Upon our screens
S'pity I usually
forget to watch.

KIRSTY'S HOME MADE HOMES

Oh Kirsty
aren't you thirsty
after all that home-making?
Oh Kirsty in your
"Forever Home"
that you rent out to people.

ODE TO HEARTBEAT

Oh the sixties! When the Beatles played!
Yesterday, Love Me Do. Oh how we swayed!
To the rhythm and sounds that Merseybeat made.
A hot sweaty Cavern, oh the heat!
And based in these times is Heartbeat.
What a lovely idea.

You may say it's not interesting to see sixties people arrested
Loon pant wearing, brightly coloured vested
But add a sixties soundtrack never to be bested
Then you got a hit on your hands
There are now thousands of Heartbeat fans.
What a lovely idea.

Old Nick Berry, playing a copper was the first to arrive
He'd been Wicksy in EastEnders, man alive!
To detain criminals he did, over seven series strive
His wife was a doctor and was modern, feminist and vocal
And they settled in despite initial problems with suspicious and sexist locals.
What a lovely idea.

On a lovely vintage motor bike Nick would ride
He quickly got to grips with all the ruffians and troublemakers from outside.
Occasionally he would allow us to see his tender side
When he would perhaps console his stunningly pretty wife
Thus portraying a broadly attractive sixties-based life.
What a lovely idea.

In 1997 Nick was replaced by PC Mike Bradley
Who married solicitor Jackie Lambert, he loved her madly.
But they divorced after her infidelity hurt him badly.
He continued the Heartbeat tradition by marrying Dr Tricia Summerbee.
I'm sure as they kissed she tickled his tummerbee.
What a lovely idea.

The series is inspired by the novels of Nicholas Rhea
And is particularly popular in Australia.
There have been hundreds of memorable moments over many a year.
Like Dr Kate Rowan's death in childbirth in 1995.
Nothing could be done to keep poor mum Kate alive.
What a sad idea.

One of the most shocking moments in the series which was really wild
Occurred when PC Steve Crane was pushed off a bridge
By the father of a kidnapped child.
Then more recently, PC Phil Bellamy so meek and mild.
Was shot dead after his recent marriage.
As the snowflakes fell,
His Gina had arrived in a fur cape at the church in a horse-drawn carriage.
What a grotesque idea!

But in 2009 sadness struck
ITV bosses, strapped for cash, did with the schedules muck
And from the line up, Heartbeat they did chuck.
No more on Sunday will there be our teatime treat
Or will we hear "why do you miss when my baby kisses me, Heartbeat?"
What a waste of time.

ANT & DEC

Ant & Dec just
Two friends that met.
Ant & Dec, do
you ever place a bet?
On whether you will
win a Bafta
with all that lafta
that you provide.

EMMERDALE POEM

Emmerdale, Emmerdale, what happened to the Farm?
Emmerdale, Emmerdale, it never did no harm
Emmerdale, Emmerdale, you wanted to rebrand it?
Emmerdale, Emmerdale, yes now I understand it.

SKINS

Skins!
You're a shocking lot.

JONATHAN ROSS

Jonathan Ross!
You show 'em who's da boss.
You're funny & you make alota money
Your style is better than Jeremy Kyle
Stay away from Brand
Cos you don't need that kinda hassle.
You're Jonathan Ross
not Luke Goss
or Matt Goss.

THE BILL (REPRISE)

The Bill
The Bill
I watch you when
I'm ill.

If you enjoyed these poems please donate some money to charity
Luv Holly

CCTV NO:1250
SUBJECT: ANGELINA JOLIE
LOCATION: PETROL STATION

CCTV NO:2734
SUBJECT: KIMBERELY WALSH
LOCATION: BASILDON TOWN CENTRE

CCTV NO:5874
SUBJECT: PETE BENNETT
LOCATION: THE LOCAL SHOP

CCTV NO:6872
SUBJECT: AMY WINEHOUSE
LOCATION: FINSBURY PARK MOSQUE

CCTV HIGHLIGHTS

CCTV No. 1250 >>>>>>
ANGELINA JOLIE filling up her VW Passat estate with juice. A source tells us she just put a tenner in – what a tight wad! But what brilliant control of the nozzle – no wonder Brad's smiling. She can control my nozzle with her index finger any day of the week!!! *(What do you mean? I don't get it – H)*

CCTV No. 2734 >>>>>>
Girls Aloud vocalist **KIMBERLEY WALSH** in Basildon town centre – look out KW don't tread in that doggie dirt, otherwise it'll be more than apple bottom jeans you're wearing – or boots with the fur!!!

CCTV No. 3993 >>>>>>
CHARLIE BROOKER in the multi-storey car park at Asda. Star of BBC3's Screen Wipe! and News Wipe! Caught off-duty loading up his Honda with the week's shopping. Hey Chas, is that an Asian Fusion Meal for two in your trolley or are you just pleased to see us?!!!

CCTV No. 4182 >>>>>>
SIR SEAN CONNERY at the cashpoint. Good disguise, Conners but we know it's you under that hoodie at the cashpoint, withdrawing a fistful of Scottish tenners – what's your PIN number, Double-O-Seven?!!! *(No, they have to have four digits – H)*

HAVE YOU GOT ANY CCTV FOOTAGE OF THE STARS AT PLAY? >>>>>>>>>>>

CCTV NO:3993
SUBJECT: CHARLIE BROOKER
LOCATION: ASDA MULTI STOREY CAR PARK

CCTV NO:4182
SUBJECT: SIR SEAN CONNERY
LOCATION: CASHPOINT

CCTV NO:7222
SUBJECT: CHARLOTTE CHURCH & GAVIN HENSON
LOCATION: THE GUTTER

CCTV NO:8520
SUBJECT: ABU HAMZA
LOCATION: PARK BENCH

HERE'S SOME GROOVY SHOTS OF SOME OF OUR TOP CELEBS AT PLAY CAUGHT ON CCTV FOOTAGE >>>>>>

CCTV No. 5874 >>>>>>

PETE BENNETT off Big Brother at the corner shop. Just 'cos he's got Tourette's syndrome doesn't mean he don't have to eat! Here is the BB winner buying his self a carton of milk from Londis. Come to the DAIRY room please!!! *(Shouldn't that be DIARY room? – H)*

CCTV No. 6872 >>>>>>

AMY WINEHOUSE walking past Finsbury Park Mosque. No doubt on the way to visit hubby Blake Fielder-Civil in Pentonville, they tried to make her wear a hijab but she said no, no, no!!!

CCTV No. 7222 >>>>>>

CHARLOTTE CHURCH AND GAVIN HENSON in the gutter. The Welsh diva and her rugby stud are caught measuring the tread on the tyres of their Ford Maverick. Church's company had £3.6 million assets in 2007–08 and her trustees have invested in jewels, shares and property. *(What's that got to do with it? – H)*

CCTV No. 8520 >>>>>>

ABU HAMZA on a bench. The cheeky behooked cleric is caught on camera taking a moment for quiet contemplation on a park bench in the leafy London suburb where he lives peacefully with his wife and two children. *(Eh? – H)*

IF SO, SEND IT IN TO US HERE AND WE WILL LOOK AT IT WITH OUR EYES

Gok-Wan's
celebrity fashion faux pas

BEFORE

AFTER

Cheryl Cole

Talk about Cole's slaw!
Oh Cheryl what have you done to your tiny bird-like body?
You got a great figure girlfriend – gorgeous eyes that wink! Not to mention a naughty boyfriend that I'd love to pass and dribble on!!! But missy you ain't showing the goods like they should be shown – no wonder Ashley's playing games away from home with his football club!!! If you're buying fruit from M&S you expect to see the apples nicely displayed. The way you're going, it looks like stewed prunes from Asda! Girlfriend, really!

Gok Sez:

This halter-neck top shows off your bust and the marker pen arrows on your neck draw the attention down towards them, the upside-down cardigan on your legs instead of trousers says I'm up for experimentation, and I love my calves. Like they say at Maccy D's I'm Lovin' It, and can I have some extra sauce please.

BEFORE

AFTER

Poshum Becks

Oh Victoria! What you like girlfriend?!!
Take a look at yo'self in the mirror honey bun! Mirror, mirror on the wall who is the scariest of 'em all?
– and it ain't Scary Spice no more! That waist band is way too high up and makes you look like you're out trick or treatin' rather than attending a premiere! You've got some great features in there somewhere. Let Gok see if he can find it.

Gok Sez:

Full-length hog's hair coat, muffler and duck-shaped trilby shows off that great nose of yours.
If you got it girlfriend – flaunt it, flare those nostrils baby!

BEFORE

AFTER

Ricky Hatton

Yo boyfriend what's with the big belts?
It just attracts attention to yo' skinny-assed hips! Shorts are no-no too little guy
unless you're on the beach in Marbella with Dale or Cilla.
And gloves? Gloves with shorts?
Get outta here boyfriend and don't come back till you won one!

Gok Sez:

You're big enough to be in long trousers now boyfriend, lose the belt
and go for something with a snake clasp, white shirt, tie and blazer
with a jaunty cap – takes years off you boyfriend – knockout!

Hey girlfriend! Or in my case boyfriend!

Did you see some of this year's fashion faux pas? Red faces on the red carpet or what! What are they like? You'd think with all that money that they'd get it right for once but no it's like – whatever! I'm tellin' you girlfriend I feel like getting a velvet rope and stringin' the lot of 'em up! No, seriously now girlfriend I have a passion for fashion and it ain't something you should ration!!!

Camilla Parker Bowles

Duchess of Cornwall? Duchess of Corn-balls more like!
What do you think you're up to representing our country dressed like a middle-aged woman who's married to the Prince O' Wales? Prince O' Wails more like, yeah that's me wailing at the sight of you, girlfriend! You are looking like something out of In the Night Garden. Pull my Iggle Piggle and kiss my Tombliboos!

Gok Sez:

Let's go for this – full Beefeater outfit with a rook on your shoulder. Vivienne Westwood eat your heart out! This says Great Britain, it says carnivorous bird, it says cross me and I'll have you. Great look girlfriend!

Amanda Holden

Oh Mandy! You came and you stopped me from shakin' – NOT!
Girlfriend you got me HOLDEN my breath! What is goin' on with the face? I tell you what missy, cancel your next trip up Harley Street and give your face a breather – it earnt it! Je suis judge and jury and je ne parle le fashion cock-up pas! Not sure about the fringe, not sure about the waistline, not sure about the neckline, not sure about the whole ensemble baby!

Gok Sez:

Full-face balaclava will hide a multitude of sins but make sure you don't try and carry any fluids over 100mls through customs whilst wearing it or you dead girlfriend! Bin-liner dress with "Bitchin'" written on it in Tipp-Ex and Jiminy Cricket-style wellie boots that show you still got a sense of humour. You is wild at heart baby and you know it!!!

Pope Benedict XVI

Floor-length white dress is a big no-no unless you got a figure like Twiggy.
And you ain't no Twiggy boyfriend! Lovin' the red shoes though, they're like Prada, right? Silly hat though boyfriend – that ain't gonna keep the rain off!

Gok Sez:

Full-body latex rubber suit, keep the red shoes and swap the little white hat for a Phillip Treacy number on your bonce. Pop a couple or two scrunchies from Superdrug in that hair and feel the power! God be praised! Go girl! Itchy coo pope or what!!!

HARRY HILL'S
Pick-o-the bill!

You're probably like me and take photos of the telly when there's a good bit on The Bill, and then stick the photos in a scrapbook, right? We all do that, right? Well, I've taken a couple of moments just to look through my The Bill Scrapbook and hook out one or two of my favourites. (There's eleven.)

EPISODE: 2,367
THE DEATH OF LOVE

47mins 34s in

A great two-parter this, and my favourite bit was when PC Tony Stamp and Sgt Callum Stone asked a local resident whether they could have a bath in his flat. Callum soaked himself first and green-thinking Tony had his water after him, leading by example as usual. All three had to use that burgundy towel – poor Tony!

Episode 7,765
"Forsooth My Lady Love"
54 mins 45s in
A wonderful bit of business this, as Supt John Heaton attempts to work out the holiday rota for the entire Sunhill Station. A massive task, especially as PC Nate Roberts and PC Sally Armstrong wanted two weeks away together. With a little bit of juggling pretty much everyone got what they wanted. Sadly Tony and his Missus had to have separate holidays that year. Poor Tony.

Episode 76,544
"FOREBODINGS OF CONTEMPT"
10 mins 30s in.
Remember this corker? Callum and Sally join in a baptism. Now fully paid up members of the Mormon Church and get free tickets to the Osmond reunion.

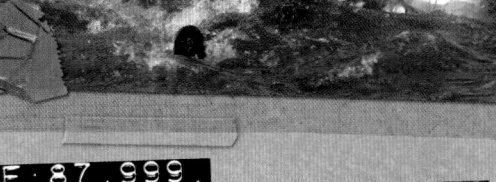

EPISODE 67,333
HOW MUCH IS THAT ENVY IN THE WINDOW...?

22mins 23s in

A real water-cooler moment – when DI Sam Nixon did her shadow puppets display, she started with "Bunny sniffing", through "Donkey braying at the moon", built to "Winston Churchill in profile" and finished on this – Bart Simpson. A great display and it received over a thousand hits on YouTube the next day.

EPISODE: 87,999.
PORTENTS OF DOOM 42MINS 54S

One of my favourites and a departure for The Bill, in more ways than one. The entire Sunhill team went on a day trip to see the Street Art Exhibition being held at Tate Modern. Tony put his foot in it when he tried to arrest 'Banksy' and French graffiti artist Le Rat. In his enthusiasm for law and order he damaged over £200,000 worth of contemporary modern art. What a doughnut!

EPISODE 878,760
"Whither The Frog Leapeth" 17mins 3s in.

The one where Callum and Sally, posing as cardinals, tried to infiltrate the Pope's highly secret inner circle and discover the secrets of the Da Vinci Code. Written by Dan Brown, with a cameo from the Archbishop of Canterbury, Rowan Williams, as the Pope's evil brother Tommy.

EPISODE: 242,529,373,635
'Quillings of Sosh'
12mins 7s in

Cheeky little screen grab, this as Benjamin snatches a quick look down the top of an attractive, yet injured civilian. Perk of the job !

EPISODE 2767,9900,99098
"The Cabinet Of Weng Chiang" (NOT YET BROADCAST)
35mins 23s in

An episode that concentrated on epaulette envy, between Supt John Heaton and DAC Georgia Hobbs.

It represented a seismic shift in the balance of power. Heaton reacted badly and after a brief tussle, barricaded himself into the ladies' toilets, where he proceeded to strip himself naked and write slogans over his bare body - such as "Leave my pips alone!" and "Down with shoulder furniture!". He was eventually knocked out with a high-powered sedative dart fired from a neighbouring building. His semi-comatose body was carried out through the main entrance, and photos appeared in the Sunhill Gazette the next day. Shortly after that he resigned, with a full pension, leaving a power vacuum that could only be filled by an EastEnders top ranker (watch this space!).

EPISODE: 982,988,727,126
"Stylish Hair On A Madrigle Of Muck"
12 mins 34s in and 42 mins 6s in respectively.

TOP: Tony leads the field in the 400 metres.

BOTTOM: Sally is a full ten metres ahead of her nearest rival PC Mel Ryder in the 100 metres breaststroke. It was a one-off special and just showed the Sunhill sports day. It's an annual event, often alluded to but the first time in The Bill's history that they broadcast it, live, with live after-sports party coverage on ITV2.

Police rules state that personnel must stay in uniform at all times and so the times achieved were a little disappointing, but Gina Gold beat her personal best in the discus.

Episode 356766 "System Of A Down" 18mins 52s in

In which PC Sally Armstrong got her holiday snaps back and was reprimanded for too much red eye. One of those episodes that centred mainly around one person struggling to come to terms with their technical shortcomings rather than a busy inner-city police force and its fight against crime. Real-life actress Ali Bastian received a soap award (The "Best Actress in The Bill who had to handle some photos", presented by Craig McLachlan. She managed a tearful two-word speech; "Thank you")

EPISODE: 898736356728289. "I Will Go Down With My Ship". 36mins 02s in

In which dinner party favourite Dido was arrested, despite cleverly disguising herself as a boy pickpocket. This was one of the few episodes that was set to music and almost entirely sung through. Gina Gold particularly exhibited a surprising basso profundo voice that led to a brief tenure in the West End in "Budgie Lifter!" the Geoff Capes Musical ("Budgie brilliant!" – The Daily Mail).
PC Benjamin Gayle (pictured) however, had to have all his lines overdubbed as he had been bitten on the vocal cords the night before by an ambitious gnat. His voice is actually that of Natalie Imbruglia, passed through a computer that changes the key of it to sound like him.

Believe It *or Neigh!*

TRUE OR FALSERY ABOUT TELEVISION WITH OUR RESIDENT TV BURP HORSE PUNDIT
PONY TARSONS

THE DEVELOPMENT OF TV

1. EARLY TELEVISION SETS HAD NO SCREENS AND HAD TO BE TILTED BACKWARDS SLIGHTLY TO STOP THE PICTURE FALLING OUT.

(**TRUE:** EARLY STARS OF TV HAD THEIR BODIES BOUND TO MAINTAIN THEIR TINY BIRTH SIZE)

2. BY THE 1970s, MASS PRODUCTION AND CHEAP LABOUR MEANT THAT JAPAN COULD PRODUCE AS MANY AS EIGHT TELEVISIONS A WEEK.

(**FALSE:** TELEVISION ONLY REACHED JAPAN IN 1981, AND THEN ONLY BY ACCIDENT WHEN A PORTABLE REDIFFUSION XK44 WASHED UP ON THE NORTHERNMOST TIP OF JAPAN. IT HAD TO BE PLACED ON A RADIATOR FOR A MONTH BEFORE IT DRIED OUT SUFFICIENTLY TO BE ABLE TO TUNE INTO SATURDAY SUPERSTORE WITH MIKE REED AND SARAH GREENE - BOTH OF WHOM WERE WORSHIPPED AS GODS FOR A MONTH)

3. THE PLASMA IN MODERN PLASMA SCREEN TELEVISIONS WILL TURN SOUR AFTER THIRTY YEARS AND MUST BE REPLACED BY A TRAINED PLASMOLOGIST.

(**TRUE:** AND IF THE WRONG BLOOD TYPE IS USED A SCAB FORMS OVER THE FRONT OF THE TV RENDERING IT USELESS - PARTICULARLY IF THE SCAB IS PICKED AND EATEN)

REALITY

1. IF YOU PLAY THE SOUNDTRACK FROM THE WIZARD OF OZ AGAINST THIS YEAR'S FINAL OF THE APPRENTICE IT MATCHES PERFECTLY.

(**TRUE:** THE MAKERS OF THE APPRENTICE BELIEVE THEY ARE PRODUCING A MODERN-DAY FABLE. THE FINAL OF THE APPRENTICE 2008 MAKES PERFECT SENSE WHEN PLAYED AGAINST THE DANNY KAYE MUSICAL HANS CHRISTIAN ANDERSEN, AND THE 2007 FINAL WORKS WITH THE MUSICAL RENT)

2. THE PHRASE 'SNOG MARRY AVOID' FIRST APPEARED IN ONE OF HITLER'S SPEECHES.

(**FALSE:** HITLER DID NOT BELIEVE IN SNOGGING BEFORE MARRIAGE AND AVOIDED SNOGGING EVA BRAUN UNTIL THREE-QUARTERS OF AN HOUR BEFORE THEIR JOINT SUICIDE, WHICH IS PROBABLY WHERE THE CONFUSION HAS ARISEN)

3. X FACTOR FINALISTS "SAME DIFFERENCE" ARE CURRENTLY APPEARING IN THE NICK AND MARGARET ROLES ON THE ISLE OF MAN VERSION OF THE APPRENTICE.

(**TRUE:** THE ISLE OF MAN ALLOWS ONLY NATIVE MANX PEOPLE TO APPEAR ON TELLY THERE. MANX-BORN BUBBLY BROTHER AND SISTER ACT WERE CAST IN THE ROLES AFTER DRACONIAN MANX TAX LAWS WOULD HAVE MEANT THAT NICK AND MARGARET WOULD HAVE ENDED UP OUT OF POCKET. SIMILARLY PHILLIP SCHOFIELD WAS PLAYED BY REYNARD BRADFOX IN THE MANX DANCING ON ICE AND BRUCE FORSYTHE BY AGEING CROONER STAFFORD 'HAM HOCK' HULLAH, WITH A PROSTHETIC CHIN)

KIDS' PROGRAMMES

1. THE FIRST EVER CHILDREN'S TV PROGRAMME WAS CALLED "PAY ATTENTION" AND CONSISTED OF A WOMAN SITTING ON A STOOL, WAGGING HER FINGER AND READING FROM DEBRETT'S PEERAGE.

(**FALSE:** THE FIRST CHILDREN'S PROGRAMME FEATURED A PUPPET CHIMP AND WAS CALLED "JIVE THE MONKEY". ALL TAPES OF THE SHOW ARE BELIEVED TO HAVE BEEN WIPED)

2. AT THE REQUEST OF JOHN PERTWEE, HAROLD PINTER WROTE THE 1973 DR. WHO STORY, "CONTEMPT OF THE DALEKS".

(**TRUE:** IN A DELETED SCENE FROM PART 2 OF THE ADVENTURE, DAVROS IS CONFRONTED IN HIS BEDSIT BY A MYSTERIOUS FIGURE FROM HIS PAST, WITH WHOM HE SILENTLY SHARES A SINGLE MALT)

3. A FIFTH TELLYTUBBY, "GIZMO" WAS DROPPED FROM THE SHOW AT THE LAST MINUTE BECAUSE OF THE EXCESSIVE WAGE DEMANDS OF ACTOR EWAN McGREGOR, WHO WAS DUE TO PLAY THE ROLE.

(**FALSE:** THE DISCARDED FIFTH TELLYTUBBY WAS CALLED "SISCO" AND WAS PLAYED BY FUTURE LIFE ON MARS STAR PHILIP GLENISTER. HE WAS A ORANGE AND WORE A COWBOY HAT)

CAMERAMEN

BEFORE THEY'RE ALLOWED TO OPERATE CAMERAS, ALL TV CAMERA OPERATORS UNDERGO A RIGOROUS HALF-DAY TRAINING PROGRAMME AT THE NATIONAL CAMERAMAN CENTRE IN DERBY.

(FALSE: THE NATIONAL CAMERAMAN CENTRE HAS NO GEOGRAPHICAL LOCATION SINCE THE LAND WAS SOLD OFF IN THE PROPERTY BOOM OF THE EARLY 2000s. SADLY THE MONEY WAS INVESTED IN THE WORLD OF LEATHER CHAIN WHICH HAS SINCE GONE BUST. THE NATIONAL CAMERAMAN CENTRE NOW ONLY EXISTS AS A NUMBER OF AVATARS IN THE VIRTUAL COMPUTER GAME "SECOND LIFE")

BECAUSE THEY WORK IN THE DARK, CAMERAMEN AND -WOMEN BECOME VIRTUALLY BLIND. THEY EMIT A HIGH-PITCHED SOUND, INAUDIBLE TO THE HUMAN EAR, AND USE THEIR INTERNAL-SONAR COMBINED WITH A HEIGHTENED SENSE OF SMELL TO LOCATE THEIR SUBJECT.

(TRUE: AND THEY CAN ONLY BE KILLED BY A SILVER BULLET, A STAKE THROUGH THE HEART OR PROLONGED PERIODS OF FILMING WITH BEN FOGLE)

THOUGH THERE ARE MANY CAMERAS IN OPERATION IN A TV STUDIO ONLY ONE IS EVER TURNED ON AT ANY ONE TIME, AND IT IS CONSIDERED POLITE TO POINT YOUR CAMERA AT THE FLOOR WHEN IT'S NOT ACTUALLY RECORDING.

(TRUE: A POPULAR ADAGE AMONG CAMERAMEN IS "MANNERS MAKETH SHOWS")

SOAPS

SOAP OPERAS ARE SO CALLED BECAUSE THE FIRST ONE WAS AN OPERA ABOUT SOAP. "BILTON'S BUBBLES" WAS FIRST TRANSMITTED ON THE BBC IN 1954. ALL THE DIALOGUE WAS SUNG IN OLD GERMAN.

(TRUE: IN FACT RUDOLF HESS WAS ALLOWED TO STAY UP AND WATCH IT ON MONDAYS, WEDNESDAYS AND FRIDAYS IN THE SPANDAU PRISON TV GREEN ROOM)

THE BIGGEST AUDIENCE FOR A SOAP CAME ON CHRISTMAS DAY 1987, WHEN A WORLDWIDE AUDIENCE OF NEARLY A BILLION TUNED IN TO EASTENDERS TO FIND OUT WHO HAD DECAPITATED TERRY THE TURKEY.

(TRUE: IT WAS SAINTLY JUSTE A SHORT-LIVED BUT POPULAR CHARACTER PLAYED BY BERNARD MATTHEWS'S ELDEST SON KENNY. HE WAS WRITTEN OUT IN A RATHER GRISLY MANNER; HE WAS DECAPITATED BY A LOOSE HUB CAP THAT CAME FLYING OFF CHARLIE SLATER'S CAB IN A BID TO CALM THE INEVITABLE BACKLASH FROM THE ANIMAL RIGHTS BRIGADE, LED BY CARLA LANE DRESSED AS A TURKEY AND WIELDING A BREAD KNIFE)

DUE TO AN EDICT BY FOUNDER EMMA DEL FARM, EMMERDALE NEVER EMPLOYS ACTORS WITH AN O BLOOD TYPE. ALL ACTORS MUST SUBMIT TO A BLOOD TEST BEFORE BEING JOINING THE SHOW. SIMILARLY, UNTIL THE BAN WAS LIFTED IN 1998, THERE WERE NO SAGITTARIANS IN CORONATION STREET.

(FALSE: ALL ACTORS HAVE BLOOD TYPE O)

4. ALTHOUGH SUPPOSEDLY BASED IN CHESTER, MUCH OF HOLLYOAKS IS ACTUALLY FILMED IN MARRAKESH

(TRUE: TO SAVE MONEY ALL THE PUB SCENES ARE FILMED AGAINST BLUE SCREEN AND THE ACTORS PAINTED IN AFTERWARDS. IF YOU LOOK CLOSELY AT EPISODE 1282 YOU'LL SEE A BOY IN A FEZ WALK THROUGH SHOT LEADING A GOAT WHICH IS THEN KILLED IN THE TRADITIONAL HALAL METHOD AND WHICH GOT NOMINATED FOR A SOAP AWARD)

NATURE

1. ACCORDING TO THE TERMS OF ITS LICENCE, IF CHANNEL 5 SHOWS ONE MORE SHARK PROGRAMME IT'LL BE CLOSED DOWN.

(TRUE: THE EU ARE WATCHING THEM CLOSELY AS IT IS AGAINST EUROPEAN LAW TO BIAS ONE SPECIES OVER ANOTHER. IN 1997 THE TAPIRS SUCCESSFULLY CLOSED DOWN SATELLITE CHANNEL LEMURTV FOR THE VERY SAME REASON)

2. ALTHOUGH HIS WILDLIFE DOCUMENTARIES HAVE MADE HIM A HOUSEHOLD NAME, SIR DAVID ATTENBOROUGH'S MAIN SOURCE OF INCOME IS ACTUALLY SONGWRITING - HIS BIGGEST HIT TO DATE BEING THE TRAMPS' "DISCO INFERNO" WHICH APPEARED ON THE SATURDAY NIGHT FEVER ORIGINAL SOUNDTRACK.

(TRUE: SIR DAVE CLAIMS TO HAVE DREAMT THE TUNE ONE NIGHT AFTER A BIG MEAL OF PRIMULA CHEESE SPREAD AND DAIRYLEA TRIANGLES)

CURRENT AFFAIRS

1. LIZO OFF NEWSROUND OWNS THE WORLD'S LARGEST COLLECTION OF PRAM WHEELS.

(FALSE: THEY ARE FROM SHOPPING TROLLEYS)

2. DESPITE WORKING UNTIL 11.20 MOST EVENINGS, NEWSNIGHT PRESENTER JEREMY PAXMAN IS STILL UP AT 5.30 EVERY MORNING TO OPEN HIS NEWSAGENTS/MINI MARKET IN PRESTATYN.

(FALSE: IT IS A MOBILE LIBRARY, BASED IN BASILDON. HE DRIVES IT TO WORK EVERY DAY AND CLAIMS TAX ON IT AS A COMPANY CAR AND MAKES HIS MONEY OFF THE LIBRARY FINES)

3. ITV NEWS ANCHOR MARK AUSTIN HATES CELERY.

(FALSE: IN FACT HE CAN'T ABIDE FENNEL)

TV WEATHER

1. THE MAP YOU SEE ON SCREEN IS COMPUTER-GENERATED AND CAN'T BE SEEN BY THE FORECASTER. IF HE LOOKS BEHIND HIM, HE WILL ONLY SEE A GIANT PICTURE OF A HARE.

(**TRUE:** HENCE THE SAYING "GIANT HARE AT NIGHT - WEATHER FORECASTER'S DELIGHT")

2. BBC WEATHER PRESENTER PHILIP AVERY IS ONE OF IDENTICAL TRIPLETS. WHEN PHIL IS UNAVAILABLE TO PRESENT A FORECAST, ONE OF HIS SIBLINGS SOMETIMES STEPS IN.

(**FALSE:** PHIL'S BROTHERS ARE NON-IDENTICAL TRIPLETS WHO, WHILST LOOKING VERY SIMILAR TO PHIL VARY IN SMALL DETAILS LIKE HAIR MARGIN, CHIN MOLE AND SNOUT WIDTH)

3. UNIQUELY, ITV COMPILES ITS WEATHER DATA BY HAVING ITS PRESENTERS WATCH THE FORECASTS ON OTHER CHANNELS AND PICK THE BEST BITS.

(**TRUE:** AND IN THE EVENT OF SCREEN FREEZE OR FUSE BLOWING IN PLUG THAT FEEDS THEIR TV SETS THEY PHONE THEIR MUMS WHO ARE POSITIONED IN KEY WEATHER-DENSE AREAS OF THE UK)

CANNED LAUGHTER

1. VIRTUALLY ALL THE LAUGHTER HEARD ON TELEVISION SINCE 1988 HAS BEEN CANNED, AS PROGRAMME MAKERS THROUGHOUT THAT DECADE NOTICED THAT LIVE LAUGHTER SOUNDED INCREASINGLY HOLLOW AND THUS UNUSABLE.

(**FALSE:** THE SWITCH CAME ABOUT AS A RESULT OF EUROPEAN HEALTH AND SAFETY LEGISLATION OVER THE DANGERS OF LIVE LAUGHTER IN AN ENCLOSED SPACE)

2. THE HIGHEST PRICE REACHED AT AUCTION FOR CANNED LAUGHTER WAS £20,000, PAID BY SKY IN 1998 FOR A CRATE OF TWELVE CANS OF MORECAMBE AND WISE CHRISTMAS SPECIAL LAUGHTER.

(**TRUE:** THE LAUGHTER HAS BEEN LAID DOWN IN A LAUGH CELLAR AND REMAINS UNUSED)

3. IN 2002, CHANNEL 4 BRIEFLY SWITCHED FROM CANNED LAUGHTER TO LAUGHTER STORED IN TETRAPAK CARTONS, BUT CONNOISSEURS FELT THIS HAD A REEDY, NASAL QUALITY AND SO THE CHANNEL QUICKLY ABANDONED THE EXPERIMENT.

(**FALSE:** THE PROBLEM WAS ACTUALLY THAT THE LAUGHTER SEEPED OUT THROUGH TINY AIRHOLES, CREATING THE EERIE SOUND OF MUFFLED CHUCKLING IN THE CHANNEL'S LAUGHTER STORES)

ACTORS

1. ACTRESS SHIRLEY STELFOX, WHO PLAYS EMMERDALE'S SHARP-TONGUED WIDOW EDNA BIRCH, CADDIED FOR TIGER WOODS AT THE 2002 BARCLAYS SCOTTISH OPEN.

(**TRUE:** SHE OPERATES OFF A HANDICAP OF 2 AND CURRENTLY HOLDS THE GOLF BUGGY LAND SPEED RECORD: 48 MPH)

2. HOLBY STAR PATSY KENSIT RECENTLY BECAME THE FIRST PERSON TO BE INDUCTED INTO THE ROCK 'N' ROLL HALL OF FAME THROUGH MARRIAGE.

(**FALSE:** IT WAS YOKO ONO, BUT THAT'S NOT TO DETRACT FROM PATSY'S ACHIEVEMENTS IN THE FIELD OF MARRIAGE WHERE SHE HAS AN ANNUAL TURNOVER OF 0.3 HUSBANDS)

MAKE-UP

1. MAKE-UP IS SO CALLED BECAUSE, FAMOUSLY, MAKE-UP ARTISTS DON'T KEEP PROPER RECEIPTS AND INSTEAD MAKE UP THEIR EXPENSES.

(**TRUE:** MAKE-UP ARTISTS ARE SOME OF THE HIGHEST-EARNING MEMBERS OF THE TV FRATERNITY, FREQUENTLY MAKING THE UPPER REACHES OF THE SUNDAY TIMES RICH LIST. BILL GATES MADE MOST OF HIS MONEY FROM DOING MAKE-UP ON THE DES O'CONNOR SHOW AND ASIAN BILLIONAIRE LAKMIL RICHTEA STILL DOES DALE WINTON)

2. UNDERCOVER REPORTER DONAL MACINTYRE ONCE WENT UNDERCOVER AS A FEMALE MAKE-UP ARTIST TO EXPOSE THE FALSE EXPENSES CLAIMS BUT WAS QUICKLY SPOTTED AS HE WAS TERRIBLE AT DOING HIS OWN MAKE-UP.

(**FALSE:** HE WAS SPOTTED BECAUSE HIS HANDS WERE PARTICULARLY HAIRY BUT MANAGED TO MAKE ONLOOKERS THINK THAT HE WAS BRITAIN'S GOT TALENT'S SUSAN BOYLE, BY SINGING 'I DREAMED A DREAM' FOUR TIMES IN QUICK SUCCESSION)

3. IN 1971, SIR DAVID ATTENBOROUGH MADE A PACT WITH SATAN IN WHICH SIR DAVID WOULD NEVER AGE. TO CONCEAL THIS FROM THE PUBLIC, HE HAS BEEN MADE-UP TO LOOK PROGRESSIVELY OLDER AS TIME HAS PASSED.

(**FALSE:** SIR DAVID SIGNED A PACT WITH KELLOGS CORNFLAKES AND ONE IN EVERY 8,000 FLAKES IS SHAPED TO LOOK LIKE DAVE'S PROFILE WHEN HELD BY THE SMALLER LEADING EDGE. IF ROTATED THROUGH 180 DEGREES IT IS TRANSFORMED INTO SATAN HIMSELF, WHICH IS PRESUMABLY WHERE THE URBAN MYTH ABOUT THE AGE PACT CAME FROM)

SUE BARKER'S *FANTASY* *QUESTION* OF *SPORT*

"People often come up to me in the street and say 'Sue, if you could have anyone at all on Britain's longest continuously running game show, be they alive or dead, from the world of sport or otherwise, who would you choose?' That's why I'm so delighted that Harry has given me this opportunity to at last reveal my ultimate Q of S dream teams. Cheers H!"

JOE'S TEAM

We have had many great sporting legends on A Question of Sport over the years, but for some reason never a racehorse. I can't help wondering how the ill-fated winner of the 1981 Derby would have performed on the show had he not been kidnapped, never to be seen again. It wouldn't have all been plain sailing for Shergar; his inability to speak or simply make himself understood would have caused problems. Then again, that didn't stop Ally McCoist being a team captain for eleven years.

SHERGAR

An odd choice, you're probably thinking – but can you imagine how much fun the notorious General Secretary of the Communist Party of the Soviet Union's Central Committee between 1922 and 1953 would have had with The Mystery Guest Round? Also, former team captains such as Willie Carson and Ian "Beefy" Botham have proved that you occasionally have to rule your Q of S team members with an rod of iron – something that definitely wouldn't have fazed the orchestrator of The Great Purge during the tense Fingers On Buzzers section.

JOSEPH STALIN

Don't ask me why, but I just feel that Albert Square's Jean Slater would be a Q of S natural. Anybody that can keep a livewire like young Stacey in check, whilst simultaneously dealing with her own bouts of manic depression, would have no trouble with Phil Tufnell! Complete inability to cope under pressure would no doubt lead to high jinx – and quite probably complete emotional meltdown – during the One Minute Round. She'd give great TV.

STACEY'S MUM

JOAN'S TEAM

Over the years we've made several approaches to The Planet of the Apes star. Rumours abound that he doesn't want his lack of sporting knowledge laid bare on national television, which for me is missing the point as a Q of S has always been about fun first, sport second. Along with failing to win the women's singles title at Wimbledon, never having the opportunity to discover whether the young chimp would have gone "Home" or "Away" is one of my greatest regrets in life.

GALEN

Shamefully we've never had a woman team captain on A Question of Sport. Step forward The Maid of Orleans! Beautiful, strong-willed and with the patience of a Saint (which you need with Matt Dawson!) our Joanie would have no trouble occupying the "hot-seat". Having fought in a war that lasted for 100 Years, I'm sure she'd take the hectic filming schedule – which sometimes sees up to two editions of a Q of S filmed on the same day – in her stride.

JOAN OF ARC

Slightly bending the rules I know because you're getting four team members for the price of one, but I think we can make an exception for the boy band that came so close to winning X Factor. Although they aren't armed with the depth of sporting trivia possessed by Girls Aloud they would more than hold their own. We'd hope to persuade them to give us an impromptu a cappella version of one of the songs they sung en route to the final – although not Hit Me Baby One More Time which they made a complete horlicks of.

JLS

The 6 Degrees Of CORONATION ST.

Did you know you are only ever six degrees away from being in Coronation Street? That you can link any other show or famous person to Coronation Street in just six easy steps or less? You can literally start anywhere and then try and get to Corrie within six degrees. A good family way of playing is to pass each degree on to the next person, so Dad would start, then pass on to Mum, then Mum's live-in lover, then to the Polish student and so on to see if they can make the connection within six steps.

Here are some examples to start you off:

STEPS. **1.** **2.** **3.** **4.** **5.** **6.**

BEAR GRYLLS

Who wears a woolly jumper, as worn by the sheep in...

EMMERDALE
Who are terrified of...

HUGH FEARNLEY WHITTINGSTALL

Who lives in a cottage, much like...

MISS MARPLE
Who solves murders, much like the team on...

TAGGART
Who come from Scotland as does Tony from...

CORONATION ST.

EASTENDERS
Which has a market. Which was one of the tasks on...

THE APPRENTICE
Which stars...

SIR ALAN SUGAR
Who he says it is in no way a reality show like...

BIG BROTHER
Which stars the kind of people who found University a Challenge, just like the show...

UNIVERSITY CHALLENGE
Which is presented by Jeremy Paxman, who makes sure he always Sky Pluses...

CORONATION ST.

My Perfect Night In

KERRY KATONA
Invite cameras into house and let them set up in every room. Chat to nanny about the progress of children. Get into pyjamas and order takeaway. Fall asleep on sofa. Wake up and try and rub cushion marks off side of face. Go clubbing.
(Er...that's actually going out isn't it Kerry? Not a night in – H).

My Perfect Night In

ROSS KEMP
Have bath. Set up living room as war zone and wait for Andy McNab to come round. Play SAS game with Andy McNab. Have a sweet sherry and listen to "Men At Work".

ROBIN HOOD
Who wears a hoody, just like the kids on...

SKINS
Which is on the opposite end of the spectrum from...

skins

LAST OF THE SUMMER WINE
Which has been on since time began, just like...

BLUE PETER
Who show you how to make things like the Island from...

THUNDERBIRDS
Which are made from cereal packs, which you can buy from The Kabin in...

CORONATION ST.

TIME TEAM
Who are always in funny-shaped holes, as is...

DALE WINTON
from the Hole In The Wall — Who looks like he's been Tango'd, which is dance they do on...

STRICTLY COME DANCING
Which is nothing at all like...

DANCING ON ICE
Which is hosted by Phillip Schofield, who also hosts...

THIS MORNING
Which used to be based in Manchester, as is...

CORONATION ST.

TOP GEAR
features The Hamster, which sounds a bit like...

ABU HAMZA
the prominent Muslim cleric who has hooks instead of hands. Hooks also feature on...

EXTREME FISHING WITH ROBSON GREEN
Who had a hit with "Unchained Melody" which is Simon Cowell's favourite song on...

THE X FACTOR
Which has higher ratings than any show on BBC2 which also used to show...

THE MARY WHITEHOUSE EXPERIENCE
starring Newman and Baddiel which sounds a bit like Newton and Ridley which is the brewery that owns the Rovers Return on...

CORONATION ST.

Why not try some of these as starters:

THE BOY WHOSE SKIN FELL OFF

THE STATE FUNERAL OF THE QUEEN MUM

WORKING LUNCH

BREAKFAST ENCHANCEMENT: A TONIGHT WITH TREVOR MCDONALD SPECIAL

HORNE & CORDEN

Good Luck!

At home with Kirstie and Phil

LOVIN' THE NEW PAD PHILIP!

LOOK AT THOSE VIEWS. THEY'RE TO DIE FOR!

THANKS KIRSTIE, IN THE HEART OF THE COUNTRY, YET HOP ON A TRAIN AND YOU'RE TWENTY MINUTES FROM THE INDUSTRIAL CENTRE OF SHEFFIELD.

AND PLENTY OF SPACE IF WE WANT FRIENDS TO STAY!

DING DONG

OH THAT MUST BE MY SISTER AND HER NEW HUSBAND. I SAID THEY COULD STAY OVER WHILE THEY EXPLORED THE SURROUNDING COUNTRYSIDE!

LATER THAT WEEK...

BOING! BOING! BOING! BOING! BOING! BOING! BOING! BOING!

HMMM! THESE WALLS ARE A BIT THIN KIRSTIE!

YES PHIL

LET'S MOVE!

JASBIR : TV's BUSIEST EXTRA
by investigative reporter Chandler Ramon

Does he looks vaguely familiar? He should do, he's appeared in over a thousand TV shows but can you put a name to the face? Well, he's known simply as Jasbir and he's TV's BUSIEST EXTRA. I spent a day following the self-styled King of the Extras around as he earned money.

This week Jasbir was appearing as "Drinker in the Woolpack" on ITV1's premier soap (if you don't include Corrie), Emmerdale. I'd arrived at the Jazbir residence — a palatial semi-detached house in Stanmore, Middlesex, the night before to be greeted by Mrs Jasbir. She explained that Jasbir wasn't there but she was expecting him home any minute and that he'd been filming with Law and Order UK as "Asian Jury Member". She was so proud as she told me of his annual earnings and produced three months' bank statements to back it up. We shared a bowl of hot tea and she showed me photos that she'd taken off the TV of some of Jasbir's work, including Onlooker on The Bill, Onlooker on The Royal, Passerby on The Royal Today, Man in Crowd on The Bill again, and Man with Bandaged Foot on Casualty.

As Mrs Jasbir started to prepare supper I salivated at the glorious smells that were coming up out of their modest galley kitchen. "What's cooking?" I asked and she explained that she was reheating some food that Jasbir had been allowed to bring home from the previous day's Law and Order shoot, vol au vents, cold broccoli and with McVitie's cake bars for pudding. "Just think of the money we're saving," she said! Soon the familiar face of Jasbir appeared at the front door — he was home. "There you go luv!" he said, and upturned a big carrier bag full of stuff on to the hearth rug. Mrs Jasbir squealed as all manner of goodies tumbled out — biscuits, chicken drumsticks, sugar sachets, items of cutlery, plastic plates and of course cake bars. "You have done well my darling," she said, plonking a big kiss on Jasbir's forehead. "You will get a special pleasure tonight, big guy!" Jasbir blushed slightly and sniffed the air. "Come! We must eat!" he said, and we all sat in front of the TV as Mrs J brought in our food. We tucked into the vol au vents and cake bars as we watched Jasbir's showreel unfurl; Corrie, Judge John Deeds, Foyle's Law, The Apprentice, In The Night Garden — the list of shows Jasbir has appeared in seems endless. "It is actually endless," said Jasbir as I quizzed him on numbers, "but if I had to say a number I would say a thousand." That night I was given my own towel (embossed with "Property of Granada Studios") and after performing my toilet I shared a bunk with Jasbir's teenage son Jasbati, who made me feel most welcome.

THE DAY OF THE WOOLPACK

2.30am: Mrs Jasbir awakes me from my sleep, I prise myself from out of the arms of young Jasbati, get dressed and go downstairs for breakfast. "No breakfast dear," says Mrs Jasbir. "Free breakfast on set! Besides, your car's here." Sure enough I hear the familiar honk of a VW Passat estate and I am introduced to Jasbir's brother Jasburton who is driving us the 400 miles from Middlesex to the set of Emmerdale.

6.30am: After a long and arduous ride we finally arrive at Emmerdale and it's straight to the catering bus for brekkie. "I always have sausage, fried egg, bacon and baked beans but sometimes I have red sauce and sometimes brown, just to keep things interesting," says Jasbir, cheerfully pocketing two sausages and some UHT milk cartons. "For the journey home," he says, winking at me. As Jasbir walks into the holding area containing all the other extras there is an audible gasp. To these people Jasbir is some sort of captain, or God (Captain probably — Harry): he epitomises everything they want to be. A portly middle-aged man approaches him, nervously, and asks him for his autograph. "Later!" barks Jasbir, brushing the gentleman away. "OK everyone pay attention we'll be doing your scene in about two hours," says the rather fey series director, Peter Patricide. "In the meantime, Jasbir? I'm putting you in charge of the cake bars — one each!" A cheer goes up from the assembled extras as a runner hands Jazbir a large cardboard box laden with the McVitie's treats.

8.30am: There's been a delay. It seems the actress playing Edna Birch is still deep in a Night Nurse coma. "Take an early elevenses!" says the director and we all file up to the tea urn. I take this lull in the proceedings as an opportunity to talk to some of the other supporting artistes about their thoughts on Jasbir's meteoric rise from complete to only partial obscurity. "I think he's wonderful!" says Maddy, a fortysomething housewife from Harrogate. "I mean the sheer breadth of the work is unbelievable, and he's achieved so much in such a short period of time." "A natural leader, and loaded with a talent for extra work," says the floor manager Viv Vivinghood. "He's da man!" says a cheery Richard Blackwood. "I mean this business is soooo unpredictable but my man Zazzy B he's all over the place! He's on TV more times than the big guy himself — Jonathan Ross." "Yes, but he's very tight with the cake bars!" chips in an elderly gent in flat cap and brogues. "He has to be, man, otherwise he loses our respec'," counters Richard. "What are you doing here Richard?" I ask. "Sittin' in Paddy the vet's waitin' room wi' a rabbit or a cat on thi' lap," he says, breaking into a very convincing Yorkshire accent. "I know me character's not got a name, not official, like, but I reckon he's called Clive Gilmore and he runs an artist's supplies shop in Robblesfield. It helps wi' playin' him, you know, to gi' 'im a bit o'back story, even if all he'll be doing is sittin' in Paddy's wi' a rabbit or cat on thi' lap." "Yes OK Richard, I get the picture," I say, pressing the pause button on my mini tape recorder, to save the battery. (It doesn't save the battery, you have to press the stop button to save the battery as even when it's paused it's using juice — H)

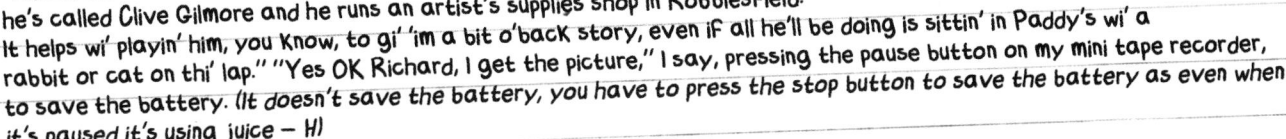

11.30am: Costume department. I watch through a narrow slit as Jasbir gets undressed behind a screen into the farmyard apparel required for his Woolpack scene. As he removes his string vest twelve packets of crisps fall out. "Naughty!" says wardrobe mistress Leah Archer. "I'm diabetic!" shouts Jasbir. "Your secret's safe with me," she says, winking at him and eyeing his fine body up and down. "Change of plan everyone!" says the director, bursting in on the off chance of catching someone in a state of partial or complete undress (Complete please! — H). "The Woolly scene's a non-starter I'm afraid, Jasbir, I'm afraid I'm recasting you as Man in Cafe eating a sticky bun, is that OK?". "Fine Peter," says Jasbir. "But we're not really going to be turning over till about two." "May I suggest an early lunch Peter?" "Oh go on then!" Another cheer goes up and Jasbir is lifted shoulder-high and carried around the costume department. "That's why he's da man bro'," says Richard Blackwood, smiling and leading a chant of "Jasbir, Jasbir you da man! You da man!"

2.00pm: What a long lunch! Three hours! (two and a half actually — H) I lost count of the times I went back to the serving hatch, each time returning with my plate laden with food. Salads, rice, chicken goujons, pilchards, spaghetti bolognaise, couscous, pork fritters, cabbage — I'm barfing just thinking about it (Me too! — H) Just as I'd finish one plate, Jasbir would push me forward: "Go on Chandler, they're still serving, and while they're still serving you're still eating — it's the first rule of the supporting artiste!" And I would be pushed back towards the oily-haired youth with the spatula.

3.00pm: I spend half an hour in the toilet, not a pleasant time, my... (Yes, can we move this along please — H) There's still no sign of any filming going on and a long-faced director comes to us all as we sit in the mini bus, waiting to go to the set of the Hope Cafe. "Listen guys, I know you've all got changed again but Edna's back on and we really need that Woolly scene so it's back to costume I'm afraid." "Do we still get the sticky buns, Peter?" "No Jasbir you don't still get the buns." "Buns!" "No!" "Buns!" "No!" "Buns! Buns! Buns! Buns! Buns! Buns! Buns! Buns!" Jasbir starts the chant and all the other extras join in, goading the director whose face is white with anger now and the veins in his neck stand out like great lengths of rope on the poop deck of the Ark Royal. "Alright damn you! have your f***ing buns you bunch of *****, **** the lot of you!" He turns on his heel and storms out. Another cheer goes up and Jasbir is given the bumps as the extras who are not involved in the bumping toss their hats in the air in celebration of what they see as a great victory.

4.00pm: Having been back to costume we are now all sat in the Woolpack ready and awaiting orders. Edna arrives, strangely small in real life, and when she takes her hat off between takes it reveals a mop of fine tight blonde curls — not what I'd expected at all. She chats to the actor Eric Pollard but all I could catch was "...and I have no idea who had all the cake bars..." "Action!" barks the director and filming commences. It's great to finally be acting and a real buzz, but the action is all up at the bar, and me and Jasbir are seated right back against the wall in one of the corner booths. We'll be right on the edge of the shot, and in fact will be lucky to appear in the scene at all! I point this out to Jasbir. "Watch and learn," he says. I ask him what he's got planned. "It's called the 'Bog Stroll' and it works every time." Then as the cameras roll, calm as you please up gets Jasbir and strolls through the back of the shot towards the gents." "Cut! It's a wrap," shouts the director, and before we know it we're back on the catering bus and feasting on another plateful of fried and boiled assortments.

PTO

JASBIR : TV's BUSIEST EXTRA cont.

Richard Blackwood joins us and slapping Jasbir on the back cries, "You da man! I saw what you did in the Woolly! Textbook bog stroll! You da man!" "Thanks Dickie," says Jasbir. "You on tomorrow?" "No, got a few weeks off, you?" says Richard. "CAT TOTS BAP!" says Jasbir. "You jammy dodger!" And with that Jasbir rises, grabs a fistful of salt and pepper sachets, stuffs them into his pocket and leaves the bus. On the way back to London I quiz him about this cryptic phrase. "Cat tots bap? Jasbir? What...?" "Ha!" he says, throwing his head back and revealing teeth. "Customer At The Top of The Scene Buying a Paper, 'CAT TOTS BAP', it's an abbreviation Chandler. You know the chap getting his change and leaving the shop when a scene starts. CAT TOTS BAP!" "Oh I see, yes it's clear to me now." "Yes and you want a tip? Whoever's behind the counter, you must always be sure to look 'em in the eye, mouth the words 'thank you' in as exaggerated fashion as you can muster, pocket your change, smile and bog stroll your way to the door."

There's no doubt that Jasbir is, in the words of Richard Blackwood, certainly da man!

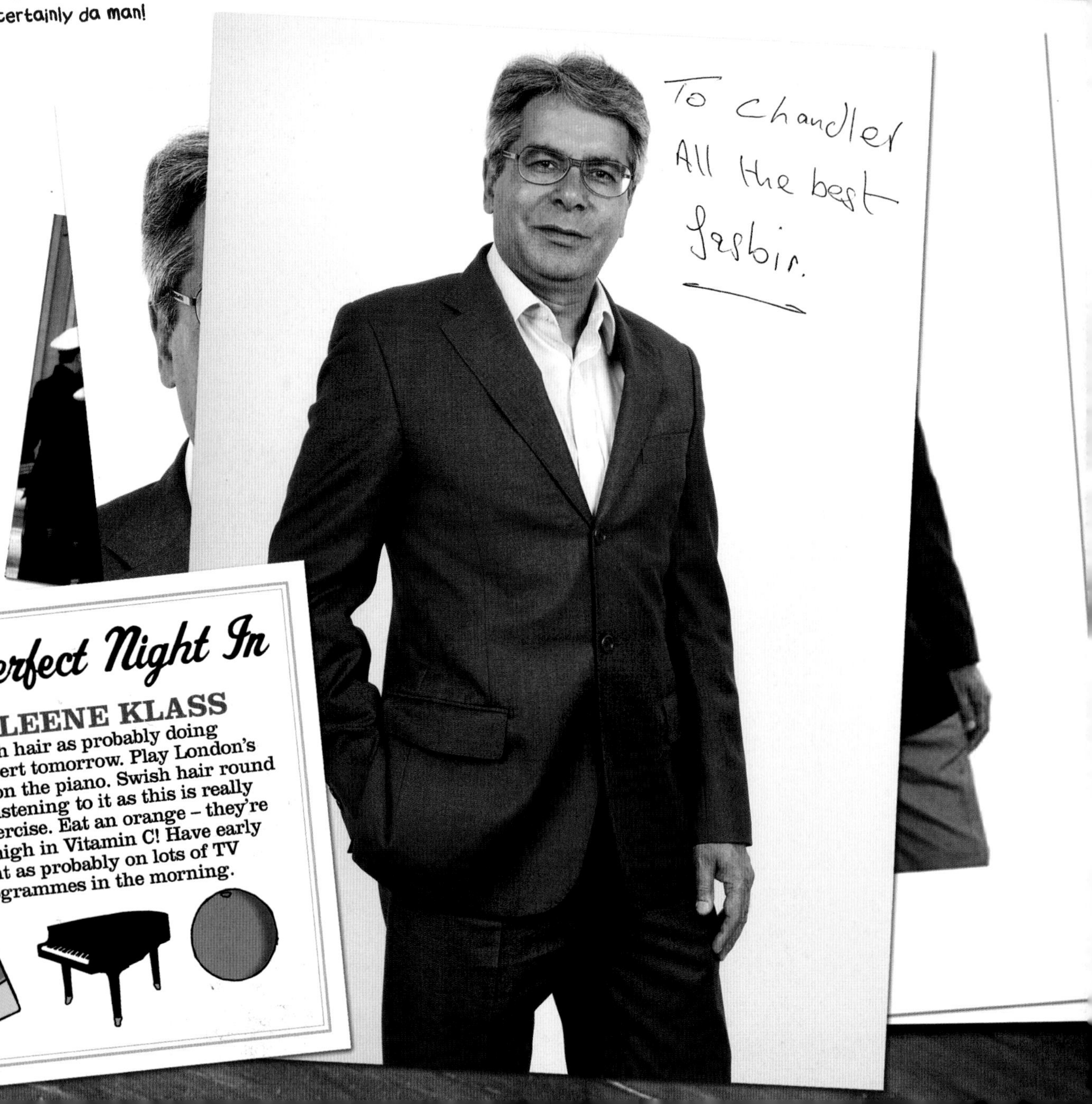

To Chandler
All the best
Jasbir.

TOP 3
WINKERS ON TV

3 CHERYL COLE

She's rising fast due to her position as a judge on The X Factor. Her winks are a kind, knowing wink, that let the contestants know that she's with them all the way. Except when she isn't. Also, look up any Girls Aloud video for a guaranteed wink. Here, she cleverly changes her wink to "Get a load of this" style wink, just for the lads. One to watch.

SIMON COWELL

2

He's a non-mover at number two, much to his annoyance. Simon doesn't do number two's. (No, literally, he doesn't, having signed a pact with You Are What You Eat star Gillian McKeith.) He is usually found distributing his wink on such shows as The X Factor and Britain's Got Talent. Simon's wink is a patronising, condescending wink, which tells the contestant *"I feel it within my power to take pity on you. You're going to London."* One to watch? You can't avoid him.

1 ANNE ROBINSON

The original and still number one winker on telly. Anne is the consummate winker, bringing a wink for every occasion. From booting the contestants off The Weakest Link, to paying the milkman, Anne's got it sussed. Anne also holds the world record for the longest wink on British TV when she had a mild stroke mid-wink during The Weakest Link. The record of forty-three minutes still stands! While it took place, however, a tear managed to squeeze out of the still closed eye – you could say it was her Leakiest Wink!!!

IF YOU ARE WORRIED
THAT YOU MAY BE HAVING A STROKE
WHILST READING THIS REMEMBER THE WORD F.A.S.T.
F - FLAMING NORA I'M HAVING A STROKE !
A - AAAAAAAAAAAGH! WHAT AM I GOING TO DO?
S - STREWTH WHAT IF I END UP IN A HOME?
T - TELL LAURA I LOVE HER
(INSERT NAME OF LOVED ONE HERE)!

HOW TO SURVIVE IN A 5 STAR HOTEL
WITH BEAR GRYLLS

HI I'M BEAR GRYLLS, TOP SURVIVALIST! YEAH I'VE BEEN IN SOME OF THE WORLD'S WORST POSSIBLE LOCATIONS AND SURVIVED USING JUST MY WITS, AND MY CREDIT CARD. I'VE EATEN A TURTLE WHOLE AND DRUNK ITS BLOOD, IN THE CAR PARK OF FLEET SERVICES, OFF THE M3. I'VE EATEN ROTTING PORK FLESH IN A LITTLE CHEF, A4 BABBINGTON TURN OFF AND I'VE TRAVELLED MILES ON FOOT, FUN-RUN IN HYDE PARK - MASSIVE, AND A SHOUTOUT TO ALL THE GUYS FROM THE ROTARY CLUB! BUT WHAT'S IT LIKE SURVIVING IN A TOP HOTEL WHEN THINGS DON'T GO QUITE THE WAY YOU WANTED THEM TO? HERE'S MY GUIDE HONED FROM MY YEARS SERVING IN THE SPECIAL FORCES.

PROBLEM: EXTREME THIRST AND ROOM SERVICE IS BUSY

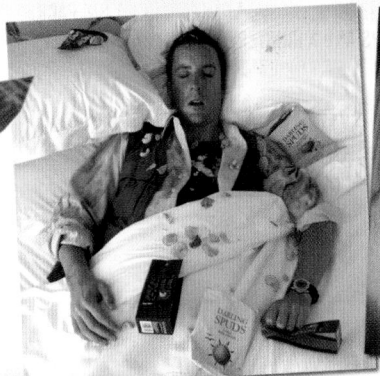

THIRSTY, MAYBE BECAUSE YOU GOT REALLY HAMMERED WITH THE GUYS LAST NIGHT AND YOU'RE HUNG OVER OR MAYBE YOU ATE SOMETHING REALLY SALTY LIKE PEANUTS OR CRISPS?

THAT'S A REALLY BAD SENSATION THOUGH ISN'T IT, THIRST? DRIVES YOU MAD AND YOU CRAVE WATER TILL YOUR SKULL ACHES. YOU CAN ONLY LIVE FOR ABOUT A MONTH WITHOUT WATER OR OTHER SOFT DRINKS.

CAMELS HAVE A WAY ROUND IT - THEY HAVE A LARGE BAG OR HUMP ON THEIR BACK FULL OF PURE WATER, WHILST CACTI STORE IT IN THEIR FLESHY PARTS. YOU TRY ROOM SERVICE BUT EITHER YOU GET THE ENGAGED TONE OR THEY SAY IT'S GOING TO BE OVER FORTY-FIVE MINUTES.

FORTY-FIVE MINUTES FOR A POXY DIET COKE?! HEY COME ON YOU GUYS! MY SKULL ACHES! I'M THIRSTY!

SOLUTION:

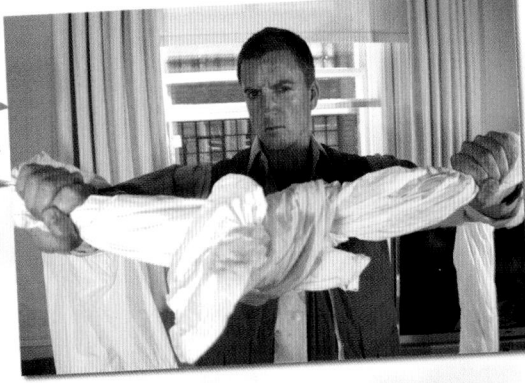

NO POINT IN PAYING MINI BAR PRICES - WHAT, DO I LOOK CRAZY! WELL HERE'S WHAT YOU CAN DO TO BYPASS THE SYSTEM AND GET THAT MINI BAR COKE FOR YOURSELF BUT AT YOUR PRICE - NOT THEIRS. YOU TAKE A DIET COKE OUT OF THE MINI BAR, THEN WHEN YOU HAVE DOWNED THAT LOW-CALORIE NECTAR YOU SLIP OUT OF THE HOTEL ROOM.

TO AVOID DETECTION SIMPLY KNOT TOGETHER YOUR BED SHEETS, SECURE ONE END TO THE WINDOW AND SHIN DOWN THE OUTER WALL, DROPPING SILENTLY TO THE FLOOR LIKE A CAT! ROLL UP YOUR SHEETS AND STOW THEM IN A BIN THEN WALK TO THE SPAR OR SIMILAR ALL-NIGHT GROCER'S SHOP.

YOU BUY A DIET COKE AND REPLACE THE ONE YOU TOOK FROM THE MINI BAR! THAT WAY YOU GET YOUR DRINK BUT AT SPAR PRICES, WHICH LET'S FACE IT ARE HIGH ENOUGH AS IT IS. IF YOU'RE REALLY UP AGAINST IT AND THERE'S NO SPAR OR OTHER ALL-NIGHT PLACE, LASSOO A CAMEL, CUT OFF HIS HUMP AND DRINK THAT LOVELY FRESH WATER - USE ICE CUBES FROM THE MINI BAR (WHICH ARE FREE) TO COOL IT DOWN.

PROBLEM: HUNGER

HUNGER - OUCH! THAT'S A BADDY! ESPECIALLY IN CONJUNCTION WITH THIRST (SEE PREVIOUS). MAYBE YOU FORGOT TO FILL OUT THE "BREAKFAST IN ROOM" CARD AND HANG IT ON YOUR DOOR HANDLE BEFORE 2 AM BECAUSE YOU WERE BLADDERED WITH THE PRODUCTION CREW LAST NIGHT, PLUS YOU'VE OVERSLEPT AND MISSED BREAKFAST.

OR MAYBE YOU'RE JUST REALLY PECKISH AND IT'S AN HOUR TILL THE CREW HAVE SET UP THE CATERING VAN. CAMELS HAVE A WAY ROUND IT OF COURSE, THEY HAVE ONE HUMP FULL OF WATER (SEE THIRST) BUT ALSO HAVE ANOTHER FULL OF FOOD, YEAH TWO HANDY BAGS FULL OF TUCKER AND DRINK.

BUT WHAT'S THE WAY ROUND AN ATTACK OF HUNGER FOR THE HUMBLE HUMAN? WELL, YOU DON'T WANNA PAY MINI BAR PRICES, AND THAT'S A FACT - £3.50 FOR A BAG OF CASHEWS?! COME ON YOU GUYS! OF COURSE YOU COULD USE THE SAME RUSE AS FOR THIRST (IE GO DOWN THE SPAR AND GET A BIG PACK OF CRISPS AND A GINSTERS BRUNCH BAR) BUT HEY, COME ON YOU'RE ON HOLIDAY! (I MEAN WORKING OF COURSE, BUT I LOVE MY WORK SO IT'S ALMOST LIKE A HOLIDAY) YOU DON'T WANT TO SPEND THE WHOLE VACATION IN THE SPAR! YOU HAVE TO DO THAT AT HOME!

SOLUTION:

HERE'S A WAY TO GET FED FOR ABSOLUTELY NOTHING. OK YOU FORGOT TO FILL OUT THE "BREAKFAST IN ROOM" CARD BUT I BET THERE'S PLENTY OF SQUARES OUT THERE WHO DIDN'T. ALL YOU GOT TO DO IS TAKE A WALK DOWN THE HOTEL CORRIDOR AND YOU'LL FIND LOADS OF TASTY MORSELS THAT MR AND MRS AVERAGE DIDN'T HAVE ROOM FOR, WHEN THEIR EYES WERE BIGGER THAN THEIR BELLIES AT 11.30 PM OR WHATEVER SQUARE TIME THEY TURNED IN FOR THE NIGHT. BITS OF BACON, MAYBE HALF A CROISSANT, A THERMOS OF COFFEE, A MINI JAR OF PRESERVE, HALF A PIECE OF TOAST - AND THAT'S JUST FROM ONE TRAY! I MEAN COME ON GUYS! YOU KNOW WHAT IT COST YOU? NOTHING! ZILCH! SO, EAT YOUR HEART OUT 1.MR HOTEL KITCHEN 2.MR AND MRS SQUARESVILLE 3.THE MANAGER OF THE SPAR AND 4. CAMELS! I DON'T NEED A BAG OF FOOD ON MY BACK, COS I GOT A BIGGER BRAIN THAN YOU! NICE! CUSHTIE! WHAT TIME IS IT? 2 AM? YOU'RE DAMN RIGHT I'M STAYING FOR ANOTHER DRINK.

PROBLEM: A REAL GRIZLY BEAR GAINS ACCESS TO YOUR ROOM

MY DAD CALLED ME BEAR WHEN I WAS KID, NOT SURE WHY, MAYBE BECAUSE I WAS ALWAYS CLIMBING, ALWAYS GETTING INTO MISCHIEF – LIKE A BEAR OR MAYBE IT WAS COS I USED TO GO TO THE TOILET IN THE GARDEN. LIKE I SAY, I'M NOT SURE, BUT WHAT I DO KNOW IS A REAL BEAR IS NOT SOFT AND CUDDLY – NO WAY! A REAL BEAR COULD RIP YOUR GODDAM TONGUE OUT BY THE ROOT WITH A SINGLE SWIPE OF ITS POWERFUL ARMS.

BEARS ARE BECOMING INCREASINGLY BOLD AS THEY DELVE THROUGH OUR BINS AND PRETTY SOON ONE IS GOING TO GAIN ACCESS TO A HOTEL, IT'S JUST A MATTER OF TIME, MARK MY WORDS. MAYBE ONE GETS UP A FIRE ESCAPE AND FOLLOWS THE TRAIL OF TRAYS FULL OF BREAKFAST LEFTOVERS OUTSIDE PEOPLE'S ROOMS. OR MAYBE THERE'S A BEAR STAYING WITH SOMEONE WHO'S MAYBE A REALLY RICH RUSSIAN GUY WHO KEEPS IT FOR ENTERTAINMENT – THEY LOVE BEARS, THOSE RUSKIES, AND LOVE TO SEE THEM DANCE.

THEN ONE DAY HE LEAVES HIS DOOR OPEN, THE BEAR ESCAPES AND FOLLOWS THE TRAYS OF LEFTOVERS TO YOUR ROOM. YOU OPEN YOUR DOOR TO RETRIEVE YOUR COMPLIMENTARY COPY OF THE TIMES AND WOOF! THAT BEAR IS IN YOUR ROOM, AND IT'S MAD COS IT WANTS TO GET BACK TO ITS RUSSIAN MASTER AND ALSO – MAN IT'S HUNGRY, AND MAYBE THIRSTY TOO AND IT CAN'T TURN THE KEY IN THE MINI BAR COS ITS HANDS ARE TOO BIG. BELIEVE ME IT WILL HAPPEN. SO BE READY FOR IT WHEN IT COMES.

SOLUTION:

FIRST UP, PREVENTION IS BETTER THAN CURE SO DON'T LEAVE TRAYS OF FOOD OUTSIDE YOUR ROOM. I KNOW THIS KIND OF GOES AGAINST WHAT I SAID ABOUT GETTING FREE FOOD IN CASE OF HUNGER BUT WHAT'S WORSE? BEING A BIT HUNGRY OR A BEAR RIPPING UP YOUR ROOM AND TRYING TO MAKE LOVE TO YOU IN THE BATH? LET'S ASSUME THE BEAR HAS GAINED ACCESS TO YOUR SUITE. WHAT DO YOU DO TO SCARE MR BALOO OFF? WELL BEFORE YOU GO TO GET YOUR NEWSPAPER, AS A MATTER OF HABIT CHARGE UP YOUR CORBY TROUSER PRESS (PRETTY MUCH STANDARD IF THE HOTEL IS ADVERTISING MORE THAN 2 STARS – IN FACT A CORBY TROUSER PRESS CARRIES WITH IT THE GUARANTEE OF AN ADDITIONAL STAR). WHEN THE BEAR ENTERS YOU RUN TO THE CORBY, OPEN IT UP AND JAM THAT MOTHER'S PAW IN IT. YOW! WATCH YOGI SQUEAL LIKE A PIGGY! THEN WHILE YOU GOT HIM THERE, QUICKLY SLIP THE COMPLIMENTARY POLYTHENE SHOWER CAP OVER HIS SNOUT TO DISABLE HIS GNASHERS. YOU WON'T HAVE ANY MORE PROBLEMS FROM HIM!

WHAT'S IN A NAME?

Famous people often change their names for showbiz and/or tax purposes. Why, even TV Burp's Harry Hill began life as plain old Keith Medlycott! (*it's true* – H). But can you match this selection of famous faces to their real names? Answers at bottom of page...

1

A: WINSTON ROBERTS
B: RICARDO MONTEZ
C: BONO

2

A: HELENA WORTHINGTON
B: GAIL TISLEY
C: METHOATASKE

3

A: GOKRAM WANG
B: ALAN DEDICOAT
C: POPE PIUS III

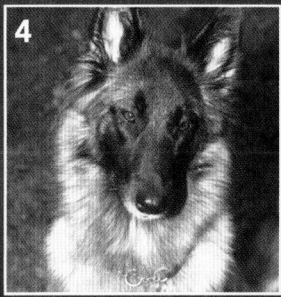

4

A: SCRUFFY
B: REX
C: COLIN WELLAND

5

A: NORTON GRAHAM
B: NORTON ANTIVIRUS
**C: $&$£^%!£)(*_$))*&%)*$&*_$^£&"^
*%^%^£$&(&^)""%^%"&*$^*(&^)**

6

A: JERRY CLARK
B: AUSTIN ALLEGRO
C: SUE LAVERTY

★★★★★★★★★★★★★★★★ ANSWERS ★★★★★★★★★★★★★★★★★★

1. C: Not many people realise that Professor Winston has spent much of the past twenty years fighting a bitter legal battle with the U2 front man who he accuses of "shameless identity theft". Despite being offered 10 per cent of the gross on "Where The Streets Have No Name" – and one of (the other) Bono's trademark stetsons, the mustachioed boffin continues to seek justice through the courts.

2. C: From the Native American Shawnee name meaning "turtle laying its eggs". She was keen to continue it professionally but was ordered to change it to plain old "Helen Worth" by Corrie killjoys.

3. C: Actually born Wot-Hen Wan, but forced to make the switch by deed poll after losing a drunken bet with Hear'Say's Mylene Klass during the filming of Miss Naked Beauty. Despite the name, Gok – or should that be Pius? – has asked us to point out that he has no ecclesiastical jurisdiction or claim on the papacy.

4. C: After discovering there was already a "Colin Welland" on the books of actors' union Equity, everyone's favourite EastEnders mutt (apart from Roly) sought inspiration from "Madonna" (Ciccone), "Oprah" (Winfrey) and "Chico" (Time) and achieved single- name fame. The only known public reference to his long forgotten Christian name came when the late canine superstar collected an international Emmy on behalf of Easties and quipped on stage: "The British dogs are coming!" – a reference to his near namesake Colin Welland's 1982 Oscar acceptance speech.

5. C: As it appears on his birth certificate, courtesy of a faulty typewriter and a tipsy registrar at Bandon Town Hall, County Cork.

6. C: Who'd a thunk it? The ultimate bloke's bloke actually spent his first twenty-two years as Miss Susan Patricia Laverty, later becoming Susie Clarkson following her marriage to used car salesman Reg Clarkson. Susie took on some light secretarial work at Reg's dealership where her love of motors developed – along with the realisation that she was a petrolhead trapped in a woman's body. The marriage was swiftly annulled, Susie became Jeremy (after quite a bit of tinkering under the bonnet) and, hey presto, a star was born!

Learn to Skate with Harry Hill

Harry's tips are even better than the experts - Duncan Norvelle and Christopher Beeny.

Chase me!

I think you mean Jayne Torvill and Christopher Dean.

Harry's Top Tips

Grit the entire area the night before. Ice is notoriously slippery and if you fall over you could break your penis off like Michael Underwood *(I think that was his leg, Harry – Phil)* did last year. It's much easier to dance on gritted ice although if I'm honest I can't dance on that either!

Drink a litre of wine. It's very important when skating on ice that you're relaxed. Nerves can seriously affect how you perform on the slippery ice and what better way to calm them than to deaden them down with wine. My rough calculations suggest one part wine to every two parts nerves, making it usually about a litre for a fully grown man but halve that if you're Melinda Messenger. Careful though, if bra tightness is not maximised women can store wine in their breasts, which can lead to drunk babies and reduced sats results in schools and we don't want that, do we? Make sure you've got a lift home sorted out though.

Gurn as much as you can. The old-fashioned skill of gurning or pulling faces for money has all but died out in the UK although still an acceptable way of earning a living in parts of Cornwall. You'll find that by loosening and tightening the muscles around your mouth your face will take on different shapes naturally, drawing attention away from your skating, thus boosting your marks. So find your camera and gurn baby gurn!

Dress up like a Black and White Minstrel. I used to love the Minstrels – and I don't mean the little glazed chocs that you get in a bag (or tub if you're at the cinema). No, I'm talking about the old gent who would blacken his face with a little burnt cork and sing songs in a funny voice while cavorting with a white woman. Once the mainstay of British TV, you never see it nowadays due to political correctness gone wrong and the fact that it's jaw-droppingly tedious if you watch it back now. Still, I remember when everyone kept a little burnt cork in their pocket and would black up at the drop of a hat – especially when trying to incriminate a member of the immigrant community. OK, so you don't see the Minstrels now but that doesn't mean to say I can't steal their style. Oh Mammy!

5. Try to do as little actual skating as possible. I learned this from Torvill and Dean themselves. Take a look at the start of their hilarious Bolero routine: they don't skate anywhere for about fifteen seconds, the jammy beggars – they pulled the wool over the Olympic judges' eyes good and proper. Even though you're not moving, as it's on ice, technically it's still deemed skating and therefore eligible for a gold medal. Nice one!

6. Cling on to your partner to conserve energy. We've all seen on the news the terrible energy shortage that is affecting the world and inevitably leading to raised sea levels, dead polar bears and gibbons and those funny electric cars that you can't hear until they run you over. So what's the point of wasting valuable energy in skating when you can cling on to a professional skater who was expending her energy anyway? It would take me a whole sandwich from Pret a Manger and a packet of crisps to create enough energy to dance an ice routine, which is the best part of four quid and in these times of credit crunch who's got that kinda wedge? No, I say make like Prince Charles and cling on to a fast-moving woman. As they used to say at my Nan's nursing home – *"Get the freak on!"*

"Way up upon the frozen Swannee River!"

COMPETITION!

Win a pair of Special Todd Carty Non-Skating Safety Skates. Available in White, Black or Black and White Minstrel stripes. Special grit dispenser at front of skates to enable you to walk safely on slippery ice. Simply answer the question below correctly.

WHAT IS ICE?

Is it A: Frozen water. B: Frozen wine. C: Phillip Schofield's hair finely chopped and sprinkled out in a thin layer. (Clue, it's A: Frozen water.)

Todd says: *"You'd be a mug not to skate the way I've taught you on these, my specially adapted non-skating safety skates. It's a no-brainer."*

Todd Carty

Hello. Sign in **here.**   New Customer? **click here.**

Your Profile   Deal of the Week   Gift Ideas

My Account | Help

you are in BOOKS

Shop all departments

SEARCH All Departments   GO   🛒 BASKET

Advanced Search | Browse Genres | Pre Order Charts | Bestsellers | New Releases | Paperbacks | Audio Books | Bargains

see larger picture

Harry Hill's TV Burp Book (Hardback)

by Harry Hill (Author)
published by Ebury

★★★★★ 152 customer reviews

Price:

£12.99
Free postage within UK

In Stock
Usually dispatched within 48 hours
Gift-wrap available

Quantity: 1

🛒 **ADD TO SHOPPING BASKET**

or

visit the marketplace

ADD TO WISHLIST

TELL A FRIEND

VIEW SIMILAR

Customers who bought Harry Hill's TV Burp Book also bought...

Clarkson's Favourite Prangs

The original TV Oaf Jeremy Clarkson in his latest video! Highlights include:

Watch aghast as "The Lump From The Home Counties" then knocks over an elderly gent on a bike and flicks Vs as he glides past in his car. He accidently spins out of control and ploughs into a bus queue of people – but don't worry they're foreign.

The piece de resistance - Clarkson, James May and Diddy Dickie Hammond racing around an African village! Watch the mud huts fly as Clarksy prangs into the water well, the only source of clean water for the village for over twenty miles. Watch the faces of the locals as they grab the grey-haired barrel-chested lad and stick him with their knives. Priceless!

DVD Extras: Jeremy's Hostage Diary - filmed on his mobile phone.

Sir Trevor McDonald Live! From Wembley Arena

All the best gags from Trevor McDonald's hilarious National TV Awards speeches.

Such priceless gems as *"What is the difference between a really fat pork sausage and John Prescott? the answer? Why one is really fat - the other is a pork sausage!"* and *"Great to see the gang from Coronation Street here tonight! But hey! wait a minute - if you're here who is appearing in Coronation Street? Robots!!!???"* and this great closer...

"My wife said to me the other day what are you doing here Trevor? we don't live with each other any more do we? We separated! Women eh! Don't they get the facts right when THEY need to!!"

Also unseen footage of Trevor getting changed out of his clothes after the gig and drinking a whole bottle of red wine in one go.

Ross Kemp In Peckham

After his tour of duty in Afghanistan's notorious Helmand Province Ross ventures into an even more dangerous war zone - Peckham, South London, in this specially filmed for DVD release. Marvel at his bravery as he actually tries to withdraw some money from a cashpoint machine in Peckham High Street after ten o'clock at night. Be scared out of your wits as Ross catches a night bus and openly uses his mobile phone and hide behind the sofa as he befriends people and marries a local girl. Not for the faint-hearted.

DVD Extras: Ross having stitches in his head and having his nose re-set • Ross having his identity stolen but because he is an actor he is able to temporarily assume the identity of Grant Mitchell.

Coronation Street DVD Special: Ken and Deirdre In Iraq

This one-off "soap bubble" takes The Barlows to places they've never been before! Iraq! The story centres around Ken and Deirdre travelling to Iraq to buy a time-share flat - only problem is, it's in the part of Basra which is not yet fully under British and Allied control! You can imagine the scrapes they get into!

Laugh out loud as Deirdre is expelled from the local mosque for not covering her head! React with dismay as Ken starts to argue in favour of democracy with a wayward Sunni rebel! And cry with real tears of joy as they realise their dream of a holiday home in the sun/war zone.

Written by Sarah Beeny and Tony Blair.

NOTE: This exclusive DVD will never be broadcast on TV, except in February 2010, then on a loop on ITV2.

Done

The Best Of Trinny & Susannah's Examine The Nation's Tackle

The two fearless gorgons of good taste invite the nation to go into a changing booth in Debenhams and have free proctoscopic and gynaecological examinations and comment on what they see!

DVD Extras: Dame Helen Mirren's previous medical history.

Barbara Windsor's Real East End

Join real-life actress and national treasure Barbara Windsor as she tops and tails this exclusive tour round all her favourite East End haunts such as the Bethnal Green branch of the Spar, Dixon's and Sainsburys. Meet genuine Eastenders doing up their old Victorian houses and selling them for a small fortune to City Boys. Visit the thriving Art Scene as we go behind the scenes at Damien Hirst's studio in Oxfordshire and have a pub lunch in a smart brasserie.

DVD Extras: Patsy Kensit's Kray Twins Cook Book.

Dot Cotton's Guide To Avoiding The Smoking Ban

Real-life smoker Dot Cotton gives us her tips on getting round the smoking ban - for instance by exhaling the smoke directly into the toilet bowl and flushing the smoke away immediately, or by inflating a giant transparent hermetically sealed beach ball around yourself in the dressing room and smoking in that, or by just smoking normally and having twelve Magic Tree Air Fresheners on the go at the same time and if anyone challenges you just be really aggressive with them.

DVD Extras: Chest X-rays of the famous people who died from smoking-related diseases • Coughing commentary from June Brown herself • Behind the scenes footage of the EastEnders wrap party in which Dot Cotton necks a yard of Tixylix cough mixture.

The Kate Middleton Work-Out Video

Keep trim with Prince William's squeeze and queen-in-waiting Kate Middleton. Kate shows how to keep the pounds off by:
• Running from your house to the people carrier, pursued by paparazzi • Running from the people carrier into Bouji's night club to avoid the paparazzi • Dancing until 4 in the morning and still looking fresh (when most people are going to work!) at Bouji's night club • Running from Bouji's night club to the people carrier • Running from the people carrier to your flat - in this way you can stay trim and spend the whole day in bed!

KATE: *Who needs a job I'm gonna be queen!*

DVD Extras: Prince Harry's Vodka Challenge where he drinks a yard of Stoli in under a minute, strips to his pants and dances on the table wearing his old Nazi armband • Special message from the queen.

Part of the proceeds from this DVD will go towards the Prince's Trust and part will be put behind the bar at Bouji's - Cheers ya!

Books For Christmas...

 amazulu.co.uk

Horny The Owl
BY MICK JAGGER

The legendary Rolling Stone's first foray into children's fiction, this tells the story of the little teenage owl Horny, who feels strong urges and doesn't know what they are, only to have them realised by a French Bird L'Wren.

With foreword by Mike Morris and terrible illustrations by Ronnie Wood.

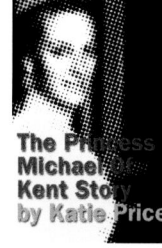

The Princess Michael Of Kent Story
BY KATIE PRICE

Britain's favourite Ash Blonde Princess teams up with top-selling author and one-time glamour model Jordan to tell her story. Written in her own, straight talking, lewd, filthy prose, it tells us all about Princess Pushy's wedding night, the conception of Lord Freddie Windsor and the difficulty in selling that house of theirs in the country.

NOTE: Thick paper and large writing.

Tana Ramsay's My Husband's Cook Book
BY GORDON RAMSAY

In which wife of top chef Gordon Ramsay shares with us her favourite recipes that her husband has written.

Jeremy Clarkson's Mein Kampf
BY JEREMY CLARKSON

Hitler's seminal work re-told for the modern Top Gear fan by the curly-haired be-denimed petrolhead.

With foreword by Paddington Bear.

Special limited edition version printed on paper from non-renewable sources.

Turning Your Child Into Your Career
BY GERI HALLIWELL

Self-styled supermum and all-round earth mother Union Jack-Spice Geri Halliwell shows how you can gain profile and money from having a child. Chapter headings include:

*"Your First Hello! shoot -
asking them to airbrush your eye bags"*

"Baby's first poo - an ebay opportunity not to be missed"

*"Writing a book for kids about something that
sounds like a kids' book"*

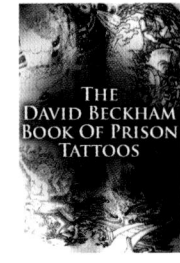

The David Beckham Book Of Prison Tattoos
BY DAVID BECKHAM

Football Spice shares his favourite tattoos and shows us how to do cheap tattoos on ourselves using a bottle of Quink Ink and a compass needle. Start on simple things like 'MUM' and progress over the the course of the book to the more elaborate 'I LUV MY MUM' culminating in a full-colour tattoo of David himself which covers your entire back. Comes with bottle of Quink Ink, compass, small mirror and dictionary.

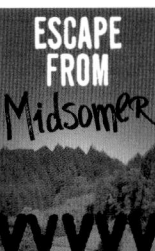

Peter Kay - My Story - The Interesting Bits This Time
BY PETER KAY

The follow-up book to the Northern everyman's first book which told the quite interesting story of growing up in Bolton. This details the showbiz years, so is much more interesting.

Massacre In Midsomer
BY CAROLINE GRAHAM

From the author of Midsomer Murders this follows ace detective Jim Bergerac as he tries to work out who murdered the entire population of the tiny village of Midsomer with a machete and a car battery. Then he looks at his bloodstained shirt and tie, and at the machete in his hand and realises it was him.
The police follow him to Jersey where he collaborates with the Nazi rulers.

Computer Games...

amazulu.co.uk

Escape From Midsomer

You are visiting the tiny rural village of Midsomer when ace detective Jim Bergerac runs amok with a machete. Contains some violence and slow acting. Not suitable for residents of Midsomer or Jersey.

Grand Theft Strictly Ballroom

You are a gunman on the loose inside the BBC TV Centre and your aim is to take pot shots at the Strictly Ballroom panel. But! Bruce Forsythe is armed with an Uzi. Contains violence and dancing. Not suitable, at all.

My Perfect Night In
JOHN SNOW

Check socks for any holes. Maxi packet of crisps and anything from Ginsters (pref. brunch bar). Watch the Channel 4 News on Sky Plus, make notes. Call Martin Bashir to discuss how show went. Glass of Zinfandel White. Kick back and listen to CDs pref. Now 70 (I've collected nearly all the Now compilations except 2002 – can anyone help?). Write diary. Phone mum.

Done

TV BURP
PIN-UP

fun on the farm!

take a look at the lovely welcome and exciting adventures I got into when I took a visit to itv1's favourite soap (except corrie) emmerdale.

we had great fun on mothering sunday in the woolpack

weeee! me and viv had a real laugh on the t.a. training day.

sorry guys! just a bit of fun!

relaxing after a hard day on set with carl and lexi

lucky I was there when things
kicked off at the king photo shoot

I miss daniel too.
a tender moment with laurel and ashley

helping the dingles unload the van.
let's hope it's not hooky gear!

giving away val at her wedding to
eric pollard. my speech was a bit
blue but everyone laughed!
may they have many happy years together.

well, I never expected to see that!
a lovely baby being born to katie sugden,
in the back of my vw passat. (I could get
£2,000 under the new scrappage scheme)

having a laugh with the dingle family.

DIRTY BOY!

Can you match the famous TV animals to their droppings?
You have to draw a line to connect them!

1
TOOTSIE
Emmerdale's Edna
Birch's little Chihuahua

2
COOKIE
(Nee Socks)
The Blue Peter Cat

3
CHARLIE
Dot Cotton's Budgie
on EastEnders

4
SCHMEICHEL
Coronation Street's
Chesney Battersby-
Brown's Great Dane

5
SOOTY
The famous TV
Teddy Bear Puppet

6
GUMBO
EastEnders' Bradley
Branning's St Bernard

A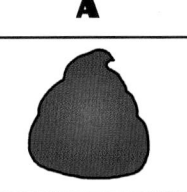

B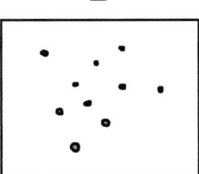

C

D

E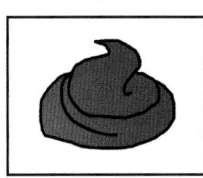

F

ANSWERS: 1&E, 2&C, 3&B, 4&A, 5&F, 6&D

WOOLLY SUSIE
SUSAN BOYLE – THE GIRL WITH A MAGNETIC PERSONALITY!

DRAW HER TRADEMARK WHISKERS, HAIR AND EYEBROWS WITH THE
MAGIC WAND – OR SIMPLY RESTYLE THE BRITAIN'S GOT TALENT SONGBIRD
AGAIN AND AGAIN AND AGAIN

POST-MAKEOVER

SIMON COWELL
SUSIE

PRE-MAKEOVER

STARRING IN
'LES MIS'

SIR ALAN
SUGAR SUSIE

PIRATE OF THE
CARIBBEAN SUSIE

AGE 4+

SEE BACK FOR INSTRUCTIONS

WHERE'S HARRY?
THE ANSWER...

My Perfect Night In
RONNIE WOOD
Drink bottle of Polish vodka. Practise Polish vocab, eat bratwurst and sauerkraut washed down with a bottle of Polish vodka. Watch travelogue guide to Warsaw. Two in morning: go down the garage and get a king-sized Twix.

My Perfect Night In
MARIELLA FROSTRUP
Phone George Clooney (did I mention I know him?). Smoke 60 fags and try Clooney's number again. Drink half bottle of red wine. Phone David Baddiel up and ask him if he's got another number for George Clooney.

USEFUL PHONE NUMBERS

BBC
They are always keen to hear from you at the BBC!
Director General of the BBC Mark Thompson: 07700 902365

BBC1
Graham Norton: 07700 9468347
Bruce Forsyth: 07700 973822

BBC2
Have you got an idea for a topical satire-type show for comedians to work bits of their act into?
Controller BBC2: 020 7946 0278

BBC3
Maybe you know someone who likes chips or bread –
as long as they don't eat much fruit they could be categorised as a "Freaky Eater".
Freaky Eaters Producer: 020 7946 0729

Does your sister have such low self-esteem that she goes to the pub in a bikini? She might qualify for Snog, Marry, Avoid.
Try Jenny Frost on 07700 983761

BBC4
Do you have some colour footage of an event that is traditionally only seen in black and white?
eg the First World War? Then BBC4 would love to hear from you.
Controller BBC4: 020 7946 0137

ITV1
If you've got an innovative idea for a TV show that involves talent/ice.
Michael Grade's mobile is 07700 952883

Or maybe you'd like to ride the jiggy bank? Phone Ant or Dec.
Ant's Mob. 07700 949637
Dec's Mob. 07700 949638
(Be sure to have your credit card with you.)

Do you have a cousin who is mentally ill but likes singing?
Simon Cowell: 07700 9385945

ITV2
Do you have an event that involves a celebrity turning up to it?
ITV2 will film it and put the footage out three times a week, plus anything that happens before the event and the after-show party.
Controller ITV2: 08081 572 389

Channel 5
If you have an idea for a show that you think could be executed very cheaply Channel 5 would almost certainly be keen to hear from you.
Reception desk number is: 08081 575 823
(open between 10.30–5.30 Mon–Thurs)

Channel 4
Do you know someone who looks a bit weird?
Maybe Channel 4 might make a documentary about them?
Perhaps they're slow on the uptake – and could be on Big Brother?
Controller of Channel 4: 08081 571 252

Channel 4 +1
Do you know someone who looks a bit weird, or someone who's slow on the uptake but an hour later?
Controller of Channel 4: 08081 571 252 +1

E4
Do you know any young people?
Controller E4: 08081 574 444

SKY 1
Do you own the rights to the new series of The Simpsons?
Controller Sky 1: 08081 573 972

Andrew Sachs
Maybe you want to get in touch with the Fawlty Towers actor who is also on Coronation Street?
Home phone number: 020 7946 1394
(if he's not there, just leave a message).

THANKS

Harry Hill wishes to thank:
Nick Linford, Adam Robinson and Jon Stephenson at Media Junction
Richard Allen-Turner & Jon Thoday at Avalon TV
Andrew Goodfellow and Jake Lingwood at Ebury Press
Grant Philpott for his brilliant illustrations and picture research
James Taylor, Grainne Perkins & Paul Randle
Knitted Character - ta mate!
Julie Hesmondhalgh - thank you for being such a good sport
Stephen Benham, Jasbir Calay, Gwyn Owen, Andy Carroll, Kathryn Jones at Rex Features, Jane Foster at FremantleMedia, Susan Wilks at The Bill

Co-writers: Dan Maier, Paul Hawksbee, Brenda Gilhooly, David Quantick, Joe Burnside

TV Burp producer: Spencer Millman

Peter Orton, Suzanne Knight, Cat Fox, Annie Gillott, Jon Lambe, James Johnson, Nikki Shaw, Adam Rose, Laura Foskett, Mark Carter, Harry Banks, Leah Archer, Vanessa White and all the TV Burp Teams past and present.

Thanks to all the stars that have given us permission to use their shows... and those who haven't.
To Joseph Clements for his dedication to all things Burp.
Biggest thanks of all goes to Magda, Kitty, Winnie and Freddie – but which is better? there's only one way to find out – Fight!

CREDITS

EBURY PUBLISHING
Published in 2009 by Ebury Press, an imprint of Ebury Publishing
A Random House Group Company

Copyright © Harry Hill 2009
Harry Hill has asserted his right to be identified as the author of this Work in accordance with the Copyright, Designs and Patents Act 1988

The Random House Group Limited Reg. No. 954009

Addresses for companies within the Random House Group can be found at www.randomhouse.co.uk

A CIP catalogue record for this book is available from the British Library

Printed and bound in Germany by Mohn Media GmbH

ISBN 9780091932244

To buy books by your favourite authors and register for offers visit www.rbooks.co.uk

MEDIA JUNCTION
Book design by Nick Linford, Adam Robinson & Alex Hobbs
Direction by Jon Stephenson
Photography (Julie Hesmondalgh, Bear Grylls, Jasbir, Heather & Harry) by Jason Kelvin
Additional photography by Media Junction & Grant Philpott
Illustrations by Grant Philpott, Andy Carroll, Becky Barnicoat & Media Junction
Styling by Leah Archer
Hair & make up (Julie Hesmondalgh) by Alison Chesterton, (Bear Grylls, Jasbir, Heather & Harry) by Vanessa White

www.mediajunction.co.uk

Harry Hill, Ebury Publishing and Media Junction would like to thank the following for their help in sourcing and providing photographs and for permission to reproduce copyright material: Big Pictures, Getty Images, Rex Features and Talkback Thames.
While every effort has been made to trace and acknowledge all copyright holders, we would like to apologise should there be any errors or omissions.